First published in 2006 by
Sally Milner Publishing Pty Ltd
PO Box 2104
Bowral NSW 2576
Australia

© Diana Lampe, 2006 *(excepting text for the projects The Cottage Garden, Spring Garden, Spring Garland, Embroidered Initials and Gift Ideas)*
© Text for the projects The Cottage Garden, Spring Garden, Spring Garland, Embroidered Initials and Gift Ideas, Jane Fisk, 2006.

Printed in China

National Library of Australia
Cataloguing in Publication Data

      Lampe, Diana.
      Embroidery for all seasons.

      ISBN 1 83513 531.

      1. Embroidery - Patterns. 2. Decoration and ornament -
      Plant forms. I. Title. (Series : Milner craft series).

      746.44

Disclaimer
The information in this instruction book is presented in good faith. However, no warranty is given, nor results guaranteed, nor is freedom from any patent to be inferred. Since we have no control over the use of the information contained in this book, the publisher and the author disclaim liability for untoward results.

10 9 8 7 6 5 4 3 2 1

Embroidery for all Seasons

Diana Lampe
with Jane Fisk

SALLYMILNER
PUBLISHING

For my parents -
May Sarah Lampe and Oscar Frederick Lampe

Contents

	Acknowledgements	5
	Introduction	6
1	Before you begin	8
2	Notes for Embroidered Gardens	11
3	The Cottage Garden	13
4	The Spring Garden	16
5	Spring Garland	19
6	The Summer Garden	23
7	Summer Garland	27
8	'Kardinal' Rose Garden	30
9	The Autumn Garden	34
10	The Winter Garden	38
11	Embroidered Initials	42
12	Gift Ideas	46

Key to The Cottage Garden 50
Colour Plate – The Cottage Garden 51
Colour Plate – The Spring Garden 52
Key to The Spring Garden 53
Key to The Summer Garden 54
Colour Plate – The Summer Garden 55
Key to 'Kardinal' Rose Garden 56
Colour Plate – 'Kardinal' Rose Garden 57
Key to The Autumn Garden 58
Colour Plate – The Autumn Garden 59
Colour Plate – The Winter Garden 60
Key to The Winter Garden 61

13	Flower Glossary (in alphabetical order)	63

Colour plates – Flowers samplers 98-103
Colour Plate – Spring Garland 104
Colour Plate – Summer Garland 105
Colour Plate – Gift Ideas 106
Key to Embroidered Gifts 107
Colour Plate – Embroidered Cushion 108
Colour Plate – Embroidered Initials 109
Colour Plate – Embroidered Initials 110

	Gardener's friends and Pests	160
14	Stitch Glossary	169
	DMC Stranded Cotton and Colour Names in Numerical Order	187
15	Finishing Touches	192

Acknowledgements

First of all I would like to thank the many people who have either contributed, or played a part in bringing the earlier books *Embroidered Garden Flowers* and *More Embroidered Garden Flowers* to fruition.

I will mention Sally Milner particularly, for seeing the potential of my work in the early days and for deciding to publish the first books.

I couldn't have brought *Embroidered Garden Flowers* together in such a delightful way without the help and involvement of Jane Fisk. Freddy Fisk also offered much advice as well as typing the original manuscript for us.

Today, I must thank Ian and Libby Webster of Sally Milner Publishing Pty Ltd for deciding to compile the earlier books to publish *Embroidery for all Seasons*, thereby giving new life to my work. Thanks also to Penny Doust, Production Editor, for her painstaking work in bringing the two books together as one.

I am grateful to the many readers and embroiderers who have kept the earlier books in use and circulation, so making this new publication possible.

Finally I thank my family for their ongoing love, patience and encouragement.

2006

Introduction

How lovely to have *Embroidered Garden Flowers* and *More Embroidered Garden Flowers* combined to form this new book. It,s such a good idea to have the four seasonal gardens together along with the old favourite Cottage Garden, and the more recent Kardinal Rose Garden,. The much loved embroidered initials and Spring and Summer garlands are still there too.

It is very gratifying for me to know that my embroidered flowers and gardens have been so popular and given pleasure to so many and I know it has helped many people through difficult times in their lives.

It is my wish that the original feeling Jane Fisk brought to *Embroidered Garden Flowers* is still to be found in *Embroidery for all Seasons*. Parts of the text as written by Jane are still there, as well as some of her delightful embroidery. She worked the embroidered initials for our friend Paddy Hornsby, especially for the book and also made several of the embroidered gifts.

We hope *Embroidery for all Seasons* will find a new following of flower and garden lovers and embroiderers alike. There are so many flowers, plants and features for you to use in this book and it is such fun trying them out. The individual flowers described in the Flower Glossary, can be used not only in the gardens but for other embroidered projects as well. They can be worked in any size or medium you wish, including silk or wool. You can adorn clothing and gifts with the embroidered flowers and create some lovely pieces.

I have a great love of gardens and have established several of them over the years and have grown all the flowers in this book. After being introduced to my embroidery many people have become interested observers of flowers and keen gardeners themselves.

My passions for needlework and flowering plants came together when I started embroidering flowers and gardens nearly 20 years ago. It has been a really wonderful thing for me to have in my life as I've met so many people through my work and classes and made many friends along the way.

I hope that many of you will be inspired to stitch the embroidered gardens and that others who have unfinished projects tucked away will be reminded of them and want to take up a needle again. You might like to include love-in-a-mist and coneflower in the Cottage Garden, and English daisies and bugleweed in the Spring Garden, Italian lavender could be added to either garden as well. You will certainly derive a lot of pleasure from stitching a garden or perhaps even all four seasons. It is very satisfying to have them framed and hanging on your wall.

My reason for writing the books was to document the designs, as I had spent so many years thinking about and devising ways to depict flowers realistically in needlework. I felt it would be a shame not to share them with others.

You will find the passionflower amongst the flowers in the Flower Glossary. Despite its complexity, it is a favourite flower among my students. It isn't suitable for including in an embroidered garden because the scale is different, but it does look lovely in a garland or an embroidered initial. We have included in this book the embroidered C, featuring the passionflower that I stitched for my daughter Charlotte for her 21st birthday. I'm sure you will enjoy reading Charlotte's Story, about the passionflower.

I hope I have achieved my aim in producing a book that is user friendly with clear and precise instructions. Take a little time to look through the pages and familiarise yourself with the layout before you start work. You should not have any trouble in finding your way around. The Contents, Flower Glossary and Stitch Glossary, will help you find a particular project, flower or stitch.

The opening two chapters give general information on materials and tools required as well as notes for left-handed embroiderers. The following chapters give descriptions of the gardens, garlands and embroidered initials. They include working notes and lists of inclusions and prerequisites.

The Flower Glossary gives specific instructions and illustrations for all the individual flowers. The flowers are in alphabetical order, with the garden ornaments and insects at the end.

Instructions and illustrations for the stitches needed to work the flowers are in the Stitch Glossary. Left-handed embroiderers have not been forgotten and the illustrations have been reproduced in mirror image.

Finally there is a list of DMC stranded cotton numbers in numerical order with colour names as a reference and 'Finishing Touches' sets out in detail how to wash and press your finished piece together with some information on framing.

Embroidered samplers of the flowers in actual size are included among the colour plates. Refer to these samplers while working on the flowers to help you with their relative scale.

Now it's time to begin. Before you start, find a pleasant, well-lit place to sit and arrange everything you need around you, including the cordless phone. Put on some beautiful music, I think Vivaldi's *The Four Seasons* would be the perfect choice! Now thread up a few needles and start stitching. If you aren't very experienced don't be put off, take it one stitch at a time and you'll find you can do it and enjoy it too. I know you will be pleased with the result. Embroidery is such an enjoyable and satisfying pastime.

2006

CHAPTER 1

BEFORE YOU BEGIN

O lady, leave thy silken thread
And flowery tapestrie:
There's living roses on the bush,
And blossoms on the tree;
Stoop where thou wilt, thy careless hand
Some random bud will meet;
Thou canst not tread, but thou wilt find
The daisy at thy feet.

Thomas Hood

NEEDLES

Embroidery crewel needles are used for most stitches because the length of the shaft and the large eye make them easy to work with. However, a straw or millinery needle should always be used when working bullion stitch and lazy daisy bullion stitch because the long shaft and small eye will pass through the wraps easily, resulting in an even stitch.

To avoid confusion, I have noted the appropriate needle to use for each step in the Flower Glossary, but to summarise, use:

- No 7 crewel or straw needle for three to four strands of thread.
- No 8 crewel or straw needle for two strands of thread.
- No 9 crewel or straw needle for one strand of thread.

THREADS

DMC stranded cotton (embroidery floss) has been used for the designs in this book. It is a lustrous, six-stranded thread which can be separated into the required number of strands. It is readily available and comes in a wide range of colours.

USE OF THREADS

The correct end of the thread to pull from the skein should be obvious. Note also the illustration on the paper band. Don't cut your thread too long. The best length with which to sew is approximately 40 cm (16″). This is about the distance from your fingertips to your elbow.

It is important to *strip* the thread before embroidering in order to aerate the strands and ensure smooth coverage when the stitches are worked. This means separating all the individual strands of your cut thread, and then putting back together the number of individual strands you require. When separating your strands, hold the thread at the top and pull the individual strands upwards to avoid tangling.

All spun threads should be worked with the grain. This is important because the thread will twist and unravel if worked against it. Run your fingers down the thread to feel the grain; smooth is with the grain, rough is against it.

To ensure you use the thread in the correct direction, always thread the needle with the 'blooming end'. This is the end you pull from the DMC skein. If you are unsure which is correct, flick or rub the ends and the right one will 'bloom'. If your thread has been resting for a while the 'blooming end' will have become untwisted and fluffy.

FABRIC

In my experience, the best fabric to work with is Irish embroidery linen. It is firm and will last longer than most other fabrics. Silk or unbleached calico can also be used for a pleasing effect.

SCISSORS

A small pair of good quality embroidery scissors with sharp, pointed blades is needed for snipping your threads.

PENCILS

A soft lead pencil (such as 2B) should be used in preference to any other marker. This is because some marking pencils leave chemical residues in the fabric which can ultimately reappear or rot the fabric. Pencil marks are easily removed by washing your finished embroidery. If you wish to change the pencilled outline while you are working, remove it by gentle rubbing with an Artgum eraser or stale bread.

HOOPS

For good tension, I recommend the use of a small embroidery hoop for couching, French knot stalks and all stitches of the satin stitch family. Also, when working French knots and colonial knots, you will have more control, and be able to develop a rhythm, if a small 10 cm (4″) hoop is used.

A plastic hoop is smooth and good to use. Traditional wooden hoops are also satisfactory but should be wrapped with white cotton tape to avoid damaging your work.

CHAPTER 2

NOTES FOR
EMBROIDERED GARDENS

Winter is cold-hearted,
*   Spring is yea and nay,*
Autumn is a weathercock
*   Blown every way:*
Summer days for me
When every leaf is on its tree.

Christina Rossetti

The size you wish your finished embroidered garden to be is very much up to you. If it is to be larger than mine, be sure you use a piece of linen large enough to ensure ample fabric around your finished embroidery for framing.

If you plan to work more than one garden and to hang them together, take care to make them all the same size. Consider the balance of colour, density and form and how they will look when hanging together on your wall.

You may choose to arrange the flowers in your garden differently to mine, making some clumps larger, or including a few of your own flower ideas. You might copy an ornamental feature from your garden, or include your own pet, a bird or an insect. Challenge your creativity and I am sure you'll be well satisfied with the result.

The following detailed instructions on the order in which to work your embroidered garden are given simply to guide those of you who are not yet confident enough to design your own garden. Read through the chapter on your chosen project, look carefully at the garden and flower illustrations, turn to the Flower Glossary and start stitching. Let your garden grow as mine does — freely from the needle and thread.

Included in each of the following garden chapters is a list of flowers and other inclusions, as well as prerequisites for each project.

CHAPTER 3

THE COTTAGE GARDEN

Soon we shall have gold-duster snapdragon,
Sweet William with his lively cottage-smell,
And stocks in fragrant blow.

Matthew Arnold (1822-1888)

Banks of brightly coloured and fragrant flowers are the essence of a cottage garden. These pleasing gardens, bringing a sense of nostalgia by a bygone era, are gaining in popularity. Here is small Cottage Garden design is massed with ell-known and nest-loved flowers. Among them, tall hollyhocks, a stately standard rose, magnificent agapanthus and fragrant French lavender are delightfully combined with delicate English primroses, violets and forget-me-nots.

Before commencing your work ensure that you have allowed sufficient fabric for you garden, taking into consideration any extensions or modifications you intend to introduce.

Should you decide to copy the cottage garden illustrated, the photograph will be a guide to the order in which the flowers should be placed. The actual size of the garden illustrated is 270 mm x 100 mm (10½" x 4").

A tacking thread outline of the finished work should be centred on the fabric. To help keep your garden baseline even, lightly draw a straight line approximately 2 cm (1") from the bottom tacking line. You can, of course, work slightly below this line with some flowers in order to give the garden a natural look.

The larger background flowers, the standard rose, and agapanthus, hollyhocks and foxgloves are worked first. A pencil mark for each of these will help with their placement and will ensure that sufficient space is allowed for the larger foreground flowers of periwinkle, French lavender and Shasta daisies.

Delphiniums in their different shades of blue can be worked behind other foreground flowers, thus considerably reducing your working time – they are very time-consuming. This can also be done with the foxgloves, if you wish.

Delicate sprays of gypsophila (baby's breath) can be tucked behind and in between the foliage. A few stems of French lavender worked behind foreground flowers give a little extra colour if needed. Forget-me-nots, violets, English primroses, cyclamen, heart's-ease, cottage pinks and alyssum can now be worked in an around the stems of the other plants.

Finally, find a suitable place to work a silken web for your spider and an appropriate space for your signature and date.

FLOWERS AND FEATURES IN THE COTTAGE GARDEN

Agapanthus	Gypsophila
Alyssum	Heart's-ease
Cottage pinks	Hollyhock
Cyclamen	Periwinkle
Delphinium	Rose
English primrose	Shasta Daisy
Forget-me-not	Violet
Foxglove	
French lavender	

PREREQUISITES FOR COTTAGE GARDEN

THREADS
Blanc neige

208	lavender – very dark
209	lavender – dark
211	lavender – light
221	shell pink – dark
223	shell pink – medium
224	shell pink – light
225	shell pink – very light
327	antique violet – dark
333	blue violet – dark
335	rose
340	blue violet – medium
341	blue violet – light
444	lemon – dark
469	avocado green – light
471	avocado green – very light
501	blue green – dark
503	blue green – medium
611	drab brown – dark
612	drab brown – medium
726	topaz – light
727	topaz – very light
743	yellow – medium
745	yellow – light pale
762	pearl grey – very light
792	cornflower – dark
793	cornflower blue – medium
794	cornflower blue – light
800	delft – pale
809	delft
819	baby pink – light
937	avocado green – medium
962	dusty rose – medium
987	forest green – dark
989	forest green
3051	green grey – dark
3053	green grey
3346	hunter green
3347	yellow green – medium
3354	dusty rose – light
3363	pine green – medium
3364	pine green

Needles
Embroidery crewel Nos 7, 8 and 9
Straw or millinery Nos 8 and 9

Fabric
45 cm x 27 cm (18" x 11")

Small embroidery hoop 10 cm (4")
Soft pencil and small embroidery scissors.

CHAPTER 4

THE SPRING GARDEN

Buttercups and daisies,
Oh, the pretty flowers;
Coming ere the springtime,
To tell of sunny hours.

Buttercups and Daisies
Mary Howitt (1799-1888)

Spring, one of the loveliest seasons, has been fully captured in this Spring Garden design. Wisteria covering a pergola, budding daffodils, scented Daphne, Dutch hyacinths and tiny violets are just a few of the many flowers featured in this embroidery.

Follow the guidelines given for the Cottage Garden.

Start by embroidering the pergola, the heavy trunk of the wisteria vine and the smaller branches. Heavily cover these with flowers, scattering leaves throughout. Some flowers and leaves will be placed over parts of the already embroidered pergola.

The magnolia tree and Daphne bush can then be embroidered; be sure to leave sufficient space for the smaller flowers below. The flowers in the foreground such as snowflakes, daffodils, Dutch hyacinths, Winter rose (Helleborus), flowering almond cherry (Prunus), English bluebells and Solomon's seal can then be worked. French lavender and periwinkle can be tucked behind the larger flower.

Spaces around and below can now be filled with smaller flowers – forget-me-nots, cyclamen, English primroses, violets, grape hyacinths and lily-of-the-valley.

The flagstones, cat and snail are the final touches to your Spring Garden. Don't forget your signature and the date.

The actual size of this garden is 270mm wide and 125mm (10½" x 4¾") high.

FLOWERS AND FEATURES IN THE SPRING GARDEN

Cyclamen
Daffodil
Daphne
Dutch hyacinth
English bluebell
English primrose
Flowering almond cherry
Forget-me-not
French lavender
Grape hyacinth
Lily-of-the-valley

Magnolia
Periwinkle
Snowflake
Solomon's seal
Violet
Winter rose
Wisteria
Pergola
Flagstones
Cat
Snail

PREREQUISITES FOR SPRING GARDEN

THREADS

Blanc neige

208	lavender – very dark	963	dusty rose – very light
209	lavender – dark	987	forest green – dark
210	lavender – medium	988	forest green – medium
316	antique mauve – medium	989	forest green
327	antique violet – dark	3013	khaki green – light
333	blue violet – dark	3052	green grey – medium
341	blue violet – light	3053	green grey
372	mustard – light	3346	hunter green
420	hazelnut brown – dark	3347	yellow green – medium
452	shell grey – medium	3348	yellow green – light
471	avocado green – very light	3363	pine green – medium
501	blue green – dark	3689	mauve – light
503	blue green – medium		
605	cranberry – very light		
610	drab brown – very dark		
611	drab brown – dark		
612	drab brown – medium		
640	beige grey – very dark		
726	topaz – light		
743	yellow – medium		
745	yellow – light pale		
762	pearl grey – very light		
800	delft – pale		
839	beige brown – dark		
840	beige brown – medium		

FABRIC
45 cm x 27 cm (18" x 11") embroidery linen

NEEDLES
Embroidery crewel Nos 7, 8 and 9
Straw or millinery Nos 8 and 9

Small embroidery hoop 10 cm (4")
Soft pencil and small embroidery scissors

CHAPTER 5

SPRING GARLAND

This small embroidery is very pretty and delicate. The flowers chosen are from the Spring Garden design, blending the colours into a verdant, subtly hued garland. Tiny violets, pink forget-me-nots, English primroses and spikes of French lavender peek from behind the beautiful racemes of wisteria, splendid magnolia glowers and branches of forsythia blossoms.

The amount of fabric required for this work will largely depend on the size of the garland you propose and how you wish it to be framed. This garland is 130mm (5¼") in diameter.

Lightly mark a circle on fabric and divide it into thirds to give and even balance of flowers. If your garland is to be larger than that illustrated, it would be advisable to divide it into fifths.

Sew a tacking thread, using one strand of pale green, on the pencil line as a guide should your outline fade. Your embroidery will cover and hide this thread.

The larger flowers, magnolia, wisteria and Daphne, should be worked first. Distribute them evenly in the marked segments. Branches of forsythia and groups of Winter rose (*helleborus*) follow with the smaller flowers –

English primroses, violets, blue and pink forget-me-nots, periwinkle and French lavender heads. A touch of white has been introduced into the garland with a few cyclamen and tiny sprays of lily-of-the-valley. A dainty butterfly and your initials and date will complete this charming piece.

FLOWERS AND FEATURES IN THE SPRING GARLAND

Cyclamen
Daphne
English primrose
Forget-me-not
Forsythia
French lavender
Lily-of-the-valley
Magnolia
Periwinkle
Violet
Winter rose
Wisteria

PREREQUISITES FOR SPRING GARLAND

THREADS

Blanc neige

208	lavender – very dark
209	lavender – dark
210	lavender – medium
316	antique mauve – medium
327	antique violet – dark
341	blue violet – light
372	mustard – light
452	shell grey – medium
471	avocado green – very light
501	blue green – dark
503	blue green – medium
341	blue violet – light
372	mustard – light
452	shell grey – medium
471	avocado green – very light
501	blue green – dark
503	blue green – medium
611	drab brown – dark
612	drab brown – medium
640	beige grey – very dark
726	topaz – light
730	olive green – very dark
743	yellow – medium
745	yellow – light pale
809	delft

839	beige brown – dark
840	beige brown – medium
987	forest green – dark
989	forest green
3013	khaki green – light
3052	green grey – medium
3053	green grey
3346	hunter green
3347	yellow green – medium
3348	yellow green – light
3354	dusty rose – light

NEEDLES
Embroidery crewel Nos 7, 8 and 9
Straw or millinery Nos 8 and 9

FABRIC
Size will vary with size of garland.
Small embroidery hoop 10 cm (4")
Soft pencil and small embroidery scissors.

CHAPTER 6

THE SUMMER GARDEN

Come honey-bee, with thy busy hum,
To the fragrant tufts of wild thyme come,
And sip the sweet dew from the cowslip's head,
From the lily's bell and the violet's bed.

Anon.

A sundial is at the centre of my Summer Garden. It is surrounded by a riot of colour: stately sunflowers, agapanthus, cheerful shasta daisies, rose campion and evening primrose, homely chamomile and heartsease. Elegant gardenias and fuchsias overflow their pots, and behind there are blue and mauve hydrangeas which you almost feel you can reach out and pick. The standard rose and the tall pencil pine add a dramatic touch. Bees buzz around in the summer haze to complete the scene.

Fold your piece of linen up one third from the lower edge. My garden is 27 cm (10¾″) wide (just over the width of this book); centre this measurement on the creaseline and mark with a pencil. This will ensure you have ample fabric around your finished embroidery for framing. Work a running stitch along this line with one strand of a pale green embroidery thread. This will be a more definite and lasting guide and can be stitched over and left in your work.

Begin your Summer Garden by working the sundial in the centre. Work the flowers around the sundial — rose campion, shasta daisies and lamb's-ear with the smaller flowers, the chamomile and Chinese forget-me-nots, in front. Beside the lamb's ear, embroider the agapanthus and the sunflowers with penstemon, achillea and petunias in front, finishing off the end with another stem of lamb's ear and a few heartsease.

Pencil in and embroider the standard rose ('Peter Frankenfeld') behind the shasta daisies. Add some bees to complete the right-hand side of your picture.

Mark in the terracotta pot and the Versailles planter and embroider them; then add the fuchsia and the gardenia. Stitch the evening primrose next, with the catmint, heartsease and convolvulus in the foreground. Work the hydrangea behind and between the gardenia and the evening primrose. Add the pencil pine to give height to your garden and, finally, work the Chinese forget-me-nots and chamomile next to the fuchsia at the end of your garden.

Complete your garden by embroidering a title, if you wish, such as 'Summer', in stem stitch, using one strand of embroidery thread. Sign and date your work.

FLOWERS AND FEATURES IN THE SUMMER GARDEN

achillea	hydrangea	sundial
agapanthus	lamb's ear	terracotta pot
catmint	pencil pine	Versailles planter
chamomile	penstemon	
Chinese forget-me-not	petunia	
convolvulus	rose campion	
evening primrose	rose 'Peter Frankenfeld'	
fuchsia	shasta daisy	
gardenia	sunflower	
heartsease	bee	

PREREQUISITES FOR SUMMER GARDEN

THREADS

blanc neige/white

ecru

209	lavender — dark
210	lavender — medium
211	lavender — light
309	rose — deep
315	antique mauve — very dark
319	pistachio green — very dark
320	pistachio green — medium
327	violet — very dark
333	blue violet — very dark
340	blue violet — medium
341	blue violet — light
356	terracotta — medium
368	pistachio green — light
415	pearl grey
433	brown — medium
444	lemon — dark
445	lemon — light
469	avocado green
470	avocado green — light
504	blue green — light
550	violet — very dark
602	cranberry — medium
603	cranberry
604	cranberry — light
610	drab brown — very dark
611	drab brown — dark
648	beaver grey — light

718   plum
727   topaz — very light
762   pearl grey — very light
783   topaz — medium
793   cornflower blue — medium
842   beige brown — very light
972   canary — deep
973   canary — bright
988   forest green — medium
3051   green grey — dark
3052   green grey — medium
3346   hunter green
3347   yellow green — medium
3348   yellow green — light
3350   dusty rose — ultra dark
3362   pine green — dark
3363   pine green — medium
3371   black brown
3607   plum — light
3746   blue violet — dark

FABRIC
45 cm x 27 cm (18″ x 10¾″) embroidery linen

NEEDLES
Embroidery crewel Nos 7, 8 and 9
Straw or millinery Nos 8 and 9

Small embroidery hoop 10 cm (4″)

Soft pencil and small embroidery scissors

CHAPTER 7

THE SUMMER GARLAND

Very early one summer morning I was inspired to go into my garden and gather an armful of brightly coloured flowers. I arranged them as a garland and, delighted with this cheerful array, I decided to photograph and embroider them as a summer project.

The size of your garland is for you to decide and will depend on how much time you wish to spend embroidering. My garland measures 16 cm (6½") in diameter.

Lightly mark your fabric with two circles using a compass or two plates and divide them into thirds or fifths. Run a stitch with one strand of pale green embroidery thread around the two circles. This will form a more definite and lasting guide and can be stitched over and left in your work.

I have worked the flowers in my garland closely together but it would look equally lovely with a little more space between them. Other flowers from this book could be included in your summer garland, such as passionflower, gardenia and fuchsia.

Begin by working the larger flowers first in each section — hydrangeas, sunflowers, roses and evening primroses. Fill in with the smaller flowers. Ensure that you have created an even balance of colour, size and texture of flowers.

Take care to control the tension while working: a hoop will make this easier.

If you wish, entitle your work 'Summer Flowers' by embroidering the words in stem stitch, with one strand of embroidery thread. Lastly, sign and date your work.

FLOWERS IN THE SUMMER GARLAND

achillea	evening primrose	rose 'Peter Frankenfeld'
agapanthus	French lavender	rose 'Rosamunde'
catmint	hydrangea	shasta daisy
chamomile	lamb's ear	sunflower
Chinese foreget-me-not	penstemon	
convolvulus	rose campion	

PREREQUISITES FOR THE SUMMER GARLAND

THREADS

blanc neige/white

ecru

208	lavender — very dark
209	lavender — dark
210	lavender — medium
211	lavender — light
315	antique mauve — very dark
320	pistachio green — medium
333	blue violet — very dark
340	blue violet — medium
341	blue violet — light
356	terracotta — medium
368	pistachio green — light
433	brown — medium
444	lemon — dark
445	lemon — light
504	blue green — light

602	cranberry — medium	
603	cranberry	
604	cranberry — light	
648	beaver grey — light	
718	plum	
776	pink — medium	
783	topaz — medium	
793	cornflower blue — medium	
819	baby pink — light	
972	canary — deep	
973	canary — bright	
988	forest green — medium	
3051	green grey — dark	
3052	green grey — medium	
3053	green grey	
3346	hunter green	
3347	yellow green — medium	
3348	yellow green — light	
3350	dusty rose — ultra dark	
3363	pine green — medium	
3607	plum — light	
3708	plum — very light	

FABRIC
(Size will vary with size of garland.) Approx. 30 cm (12″) square embroidery linen

NEEDLES
Embroidery crewel Nos 7, 8 and 9
Straw or millinery Nos 8 and 9

Small embroidery hoop 10 cm (4″)
Soft pencil and small embroidery scissors

CHAPTER 8

'KARDINAL' ROSE GARDEN

The Kardinal is a delightful bright red rose that flowers profusely over the summer months. Surrounded by gorgeous purples and pinks and the touch of gold of the heartsease, the 'Kardinal' Rose Garden, will give you the pleasure of summer all year round.

Wash and press the fabric. Fold the linen up one third from the lower edge. This garden is 17.5cm (7") long; centre this measurement on the crease line and mark the ends with a pencil. This will ensure you have ample fabric around the finished embroidery for framing. Work a small running stitch between the pencil marks and along the crease line with one strand of 471. This will form a lasting guide for the ground and can be stitched over and left in your work.

Lightly draw the rose branches freehand with a sharp 2B pencil or place a photocopy of the design onto a light-box or tape to a sunlit window. Position the fabric over the design and trace with the pencil.

As you work, follow the individual instructions for each plant and use the colour photograph as a guide to help you position the flowers and leaves in the design.

Work rose branches first and then the roses, buds and leaves. Stitch the ajuga and English daisies in front of the rose with the lavender and heartsease to the side. Add coneflowers behind the lavender. Work love-in-a-mist on the other side of the rose with primroses in front and pinks at the end.

Finishing

The work can be personalised by adding another flower or an insect to the design. It can also be signed in stem stitch or backstitch using one strand of pale green thread.

The back of the work should be tidied up ensuring there are no tags, which could show through when framed. The piece can then be hand-washed in cool water with soft soap. Don't soak or leave wet, as some deeply shaded threads might bleed. Rinse well, but don't wring, as creases can be hard to remove.

The embroidery is then placed face down on a towel, overlaid with a pressing cloth and carefully pressed with a hot iron until dry, taking care not to scorch it.

The finished embroidery can then be taken to a good framer who knows the correct way to frame needlework. The framer will help choose a frame to enhance the design.

FLOWERS AND FEATURES IN THE 'KARDINAL' ROSE GARDEN

Bugleweed or Blue Bugle
English daisies
Pinks
Coneflower
Italian Lavender

Love-in-a-mist
Rose of Mexico or Pink Evening Primrose
'Kardinal' Rosa X
Heartsease or Johnny-jump-up

REQUIREMENTS

THREADS

208	lavender very dark
210	lavender medium
211	lavender light
223	shell pink light
224	shell pink very light
316	antique mauve medium
327	violet very dark
333	blue violet very dark
400	mahogany dark
444	lemon dark
445	lemon light
469	avocado green
471	avocado green very light
503	blue green medium
522	fern green
550	violet very dark
611	drab brown dark
726	topaz light
727	topaz very light
793	cornflower blue medium
814	garnet dark

815   garnet medium
936   avocado green very dark
3041   antique violet medium
3051   green grey dark
3346   hunter green
3347   yellow green medium
3363   pine green medium
3685   mauve dark
3687   mauve
3689   mauve light
3722   shell pink medium
3726   antique mauve dark
3740   antique violet dark
blanc neige

NEEDLES
No 8 crewel needle (for 2 strands thread)
No 8 straw needle (for bullion stitch)
No 9 crewel needle (for 1 strand thread)

Embroidery linen 40cm x 30cm (16" x 12")
2B pencil
Small embroidery hoop 10cm (4")
Embroidery scissors

CHAPTER 9

THE AUTUMN GARDEN

Fall, leaves, fall; die, flowers, away;
Lengthen night and shorten day:
Every leaf speaks bliss to me
Fluttering from the autumn tree.

Emily Brontë

Autumn is my favourite season: the ornamental grape with its russet and scarlet leaves trails over the arch, the fallen leaves below capturing the essence of Autumn. There is still so much beauty in an Autumn garden. The agapanthus flowers and roses have faded leaving the ripening and mature seed heads. The cooler air has turned the Summer hydrangea flowers to lovely soft hues of pink and green. Perennials such as chrysanthemums, daisies and dainty Japanese anemones add colour to the garden as do the delicate bulbs colchicum, Autumn crocus and nerines. A butterfly flits above the Autumn garden to complete the setting.

Fold your piece of linen up one third from the lower edge. My garden is 27 cm (10¾″) wide (just over the width of this book); centre this measurement on the crease line and mark with a pencil. This will ensure you have ample fabric around your finished embroidery for framing.

Work a running stitch along this line with one strand of a pale green embroidery thread. This will form a more definite and lasting guide and can be stitched over and left in your work.

To begin, pencil in the arch and the tub. When you have completed stitching these, add the grapevine and the kumquat tree and commence work on the ornamental grape leaves. Mark the hydrangea flowers and leaves and start to work on these to build up the bush. I recommend you use a small hoop for the flowers. Rather than stitching all the leaves on the ornamental grape or the entire hydrangea at one time, alternate working on them with some of the flowers in the foreground for variety.

Next, stitch the colchicum beside the tub and, leaving a space, add the Autumn agapanthus. Tuck chamomile in between the colchicum and the agapanthus with the chrysanthemum (daisy) behind, and behind these add some stems of Easter daisy (*Aster amellus*). To complete this side of the garden fill the tub with alyssum with a little on the ground alongside, in front of the colchicum. Stitch some cyclamen on the other side of the tub and at the end next to the agapanthus.

Between the hydrangea and the arch, work the nerines, chrysanthemum (button) and Easter daisies (*Aster sp.*). Add some Autumn crocus and cyclamen in front, with rosehips, Japanese anemone and French lavender behind. To finish your picture, embroider colchicum and chamomile at the end next to the hydrangea and add the butterfly.

Complete your garden by embroidering a title, if you wish, such as 'Autumn', in stem stitch, with one strand of embroidery thread. Sign and date your work.

FLOWERS AND FEATURES IN THE AUTUMN GARDEN

agapanthus	chrysanthemum (button)	Easter daisy (*Aster amellus*)	Japanese anemone	rosehips
alyssum	chrysanthemum (daisy)	Easter daisy (*Aster sp.*)	kumquat	butterfly
Autumn crocus	colchicum	French lavender	nerine	arch
chamomile	cyclamen	hydrangea	ornamental grape	tub

PREREQUISITES FOR AUTUMN GARDEN

THREADS

ecru

208	lavender — very dark
210	lavender — dark
211	lavender — light
221	shell pink — dark
223	shell pink — medium
307	lemon
319	pistachio green — very dark
347	salmon — dark
349	coral — dark
356	terracotta — medium
444	lemon — dark
470	avocado green — light
472	avocado green — ultra light
501	blue green — dark
503	blue green — medium
552	violet — medium
553	violet
554	violet — light
603	cranberry
604	cranberry — light
611	drab brown — dark
612	drab brown — medium
640	beige grey — very dark
725	topaz
726	topaz — light
727	topaz — very light
731	olive green — dark
741	tangerine — medium

742   tangerine — light
758   terracotta — light
772   pine green — light
783   Christmas gold
839   beige brown — dark
840   beige brown — medium
937   avocado green — medium
973   lemon — dark
3013   khaki green — light
3051   green grey — dark
3053   green grey
3346   hunter green
3347   yellow green — medium
3348   yellow green — light
3362   pine green — dark
3363   pine green — medium
3609   plum — ultra light
3689   mauve — light

FABRIC
45 cm x 27 cm (18″ x 10¾″) embroidery linen

NEEDLES
Embroidery crewel Nos 7, 8 and 9
Straw or millinery No 8

Small embroidery hoop 10 cm (4″)

Soft pencil and small embroidery scissors

CHAPTER 10

THE WINTER GARDEN

Brother, Joy to you
I've brought some snowdrops; only just a few,
But quite enough to prove the world awake,
Cheerful and hopeful in the frosty dew
And for the pale sun's sake.

Christina Rossetti

Surprisingly, the Winter garden reveals an abundance of colour. The crimson foliage of the nandina and the berries of the cotoneaster illustrate this. The herbaceous border is alive with early bulbs and perennials: jonquils, snowflakes, iris, primulas, polyanthus, violets, bergenia and wallflowers. The background is dominated by a bare silver birch, an elegant garrya with its tassles and a showy wattle, heavily laden with golden blossoms. The heady fragrance of the Daphne, jonquils and violets pierce the cool, crisp air and give promise of warmer days ahead.

Fold your piece of linen up one third from the lower edge. My garden is 27 cm (10¾″) wide (just over the width of this book); centre this measurement on the crease line and mark with a pencil. This will ensure you have ample fabric around your finished embroidery for framing. Work a running stitch along this line with one strand of a pale green embroidery thread. This will form a more definite and lasting guide and can be stitched over and left in your work.

On completing my Winter Garden, I was not entirely happy with the balance of the composition. I wished I could move the Daphne over a little towards the centre and swap the positions of the jonquils so the yellow ones were not so close to the wattle. You can make these changes and, of course, any others you wish. Consider how much more striking three overlapping silver birches would be than just one.

To begin, pencil in and work the silver birch tree in the centre of your picture. Mark the wattle tree and embroider the trunk and major branches and minor branches and foliage. Start work on the blossom. As there are myriad French knots on the wattle tree, work a small branch at a time, alternating work on other flowers, to make it more interesting for yourself.

Embroider the bulbs next — Winter iris, jonquils and snowflakes. Pencil in the branches of the Daphne and the outline of the garrya; work these shrubs. Fill in the spaces between the bulbs with Winter roses, primula, wallflower, bergenia and polyanthus. The nandina, diosma and cotoneaster are added behind this border of bulbs and perennials, with the violets in the foreground and at the end of your garden.

Complete your garden by embroidering a title, if you wish, such as 'Winter' in stem stitch, with one strand of embroidery thread. Sign and date your work.

FLOWERS AND FEATURES IN THE WINTER GARDEN

bergenia	nandina	wallflower
cotoneaster horizontalis	polyanthus (blue)	wattle
Daphne	polyanthus (yellow)	Winter iris
diosma	primula	Winter rose (pink)
garrya	silver birch	Winter rose (white)
jonquil (cream)	snowflake	
jonquil (yellow)	violet	

PREREQUISITES FOR WINTER GARDEN

THREADS

blanc neige/white

209	lavender — dark
223	shell pink — light
307	lemon
316	antique mauve — medium
327	violet — very dark
340	blue violet — medium
347	salmon — very dark
445	lemon — light
469	avocado green
470	avocado green — light
471	avocado green — very light
472	avocado green — ultra light
524	fern green — very light
553	violet
605	cranberry — very light
611	drab brown — dark
613	drab brown — light
741	tangerine — medium
743	yellow — medium
746	off white
762	pearl grey — very light
778	antique mauve — very light
840	beige brown — medium
937	avocado green — medium
987	forest green — dark
3013	khaki green — light
3051	green grey — dark
3052	green grey — medium

3064   sportsman flesh — very dark
3328   salmon — dark
3346   hunter green
3347   yellow green — medium
3363   pine geen — medium
3609   plum — ultra light
3721   shell pink — dark
3740   antique violet — dark
3787   brown grey — dark

FABRIC
45 cm x 27 cm (18″ x 10¾″) embroidery linen

NEEDLES
Embroidery crewel Nos 7, 8 and 9
Straw or millinery No 8

Small embroidery hoop 10 cm (4″)

Soft pencil and small embroidery scissors

CHAPTER 11

EMBROIDERED INITIALS

Embroidered initials make excellent personalised gifts. They can be used in many ways: as a framed picture or as the cover of a special book or album. On a smaller scale, two or more initials look delightful worked on the top of a very special sewing box.

Many books contain outlines of monograms or initials that are suitable for flower embroidery. There are two alphabets presented here which you can use for framed embroideries and other pieces. The letters can be enlarged depending on the size you choose to work.

Begin by tracing your chosen initial in a heavy outline on transparent paper; put your fabric, cut to generous proportions, over the paper and place them both over a light-box.

A light-box can be improvised by shining a lamp under a glass-topped table or a sheet of glass placed on two pillars of books.

Re-trace the initial on to the fabric with a soft lead pencil. Run a fine tacking thread (using one strand of a pale shade of green) over the out-line. Should your pencil outline fade during working, your thread will be a guide, and will be covered subsequently by the embroidered work.

With the exception of the French lavender stems, only flower heads and leaves have been worked in the initial illustrated. A pleasing balance is obtained by grouping larger flower heads such as hollyhocks or agapanthus on the long axis of the letter, graduating to smaller flowers at the ends. French lavender is ideal for the end of an initial, as the stems will fan to create a fern-like effect. Additional leaves and French knots will achieve a soft, glowing line.

Colour balance is important, but as there are many flowers from which to choose, this should not be a problem. Should an area appear a little subdued, small flower heads such as forget-me-nots, English primroses or violets can be tucked into add more colour.

A N M M N W J J Y P

H K I J T F P B F

R 2 X Y U S L F

G C E O D A V Z

A B C D E F G

H I J K L M N

O P Q R S T U

V W X Y Z

CHAPTER 12

GIFT IDEAS

There is an art in giving. For most occasions, a handmade gift is received with pleasure. Perhaps it is the appreciation of the many hours of work involved or the very personal nature of the gift, for often the person giving gains as much pleasure as the recipient. Framed embroidered gardens are wonderful wedding gifts and lasting treasures.

A wealth of articles can be created using the flowers and techniques described in this book. A few ideas include: toddler's overalls, the bib embellished with hollyhocks, Shasta daisies and forger-me-nots; or baby singlets sprinkled with the simplest of flowers or more sophisticated sprays of lavender; small felt teddy bears with delicate flowers embroidered across their fat tunnies; a pair of pique baby shoes tied with silk ribbons and adorned with clusters of forger-me-nots; a fabric sewing box, the lid embroidered with a garden; a paperweight enclosing a miniature garden embroidered on white pure silk.

All of these could be pleasing gifts, and all incorporate a small selection of garden flower embroidery. Plate No. xx shows items that you may be tempted to make. A key to these items can be found accompanying the colour section. Hopefully, they will encourage you to develop your own ideas.

EMBROIDERED PULLOVER

Using a large tapestry needle and DMC tapestry wool, this design was embroidered on a store purchased Shetland pullover with some simplified versions of the garden flowers. When working on loosely woven fabrics such as this, care needs to be taken not to pull the embroidery thread too tightly.

SEWING BASKETS

Many natural-can baskets, spray-painted in pastel colours, lend themselves perfectly to sewing baskets. They look particularly attractive with the added interest of an embroidered base or lid.

HANDKERCHIEFS

Linen handkerchiefs are useful for putting inside Christmas and birthday cards, and are always special gifts. They become something special when the corners are embroidered with fine sprays of lavender, circles of forget-me-nots or small bouquets of mixed flowers.

CUSHIONS

We all love the luxury of beautiful down-filled cushions. They make lovely gifts when matched to the décor of a room. One of those illustrated is made with moire taffeta and embellished with a circle of garden flowers. It is embroidered in six strands of thread, using a No 3 straw or millinery needle. The bow is worked in satin stitch.

Scrumptious is the only word to describe the other small cushion. Flowers have been embroidered on off-white silk and surrounded by a froth of lace.

TOWELS

Guest towels made from towelling are a practical gift, but, when embroidered their appearance is considerably enhanced. For ease of working, choose towels with a heavy woven band across the bottom. Six strands of thread are used with a No 3 straw or millinery needle. A matching set comprising bath towel, hand towel and face-washer for the guest bathroom make a lovely present.

LAVENDER SACHETS

Little embroidered sachets filled with lavender or pot-pourri and tied with ribbons are always welcome. A variety of fabrics can be used.

COATHANGERS

These are luxury gifts. The one illustrated has been embroidered on homespun fabric with a small, finely worked garden.

PINCUSHIONS

Embroiderers need pincushions but not all can boast lovely hexagonal one embroidered in the centre. Fill them firmly with toy wadding. Of you feel they are too special merely for pins, use them on a dressing-table to hold brooches.

BROOCHES

Small silver and gold brooches suitable for insertion of embroidery can be purchased at most needlework and craft shops.

Key to Cottage Garden

1 Agapanthus
2 Alyssum
3 Cottage Pinks
4 Cyclamen
5 Delphinium
6 English Primrose
7 Forget-me-nots
8 Foxglove
9 French Lavender
10 Gypsophila
11 Hearts-ease
12 Hollyhock
13 Periwinkle
14 Rose
15 Shasta Daisy
16 Violet

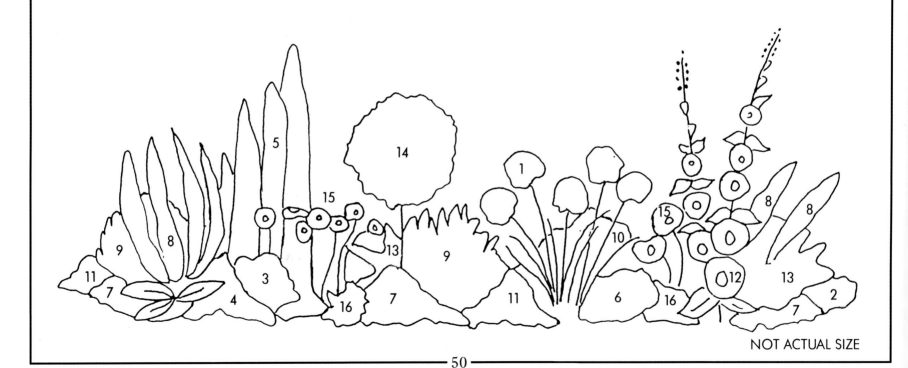

NOT ACTUAL SIZE

Spring

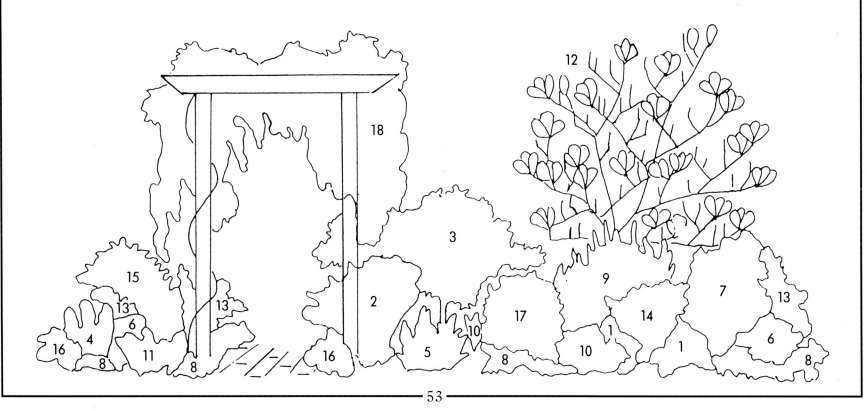

Key to Spring Garden

1 Cyclamen
2 Daffodil
3 Daphne
4 Dutch Hyacinth
5 English Bluebell
6 English Primrose
7 Flowering Almond Cherry
8 Forget-me-nots
9 French Lavender

10 Grape Hyacinth
11 Lily-of-the-valley
12 Magnolia
13 Periwinkle
14 Snowflake
15 Solomon's Seal
16 Violet
17 Winter Rose
18 Wisteria

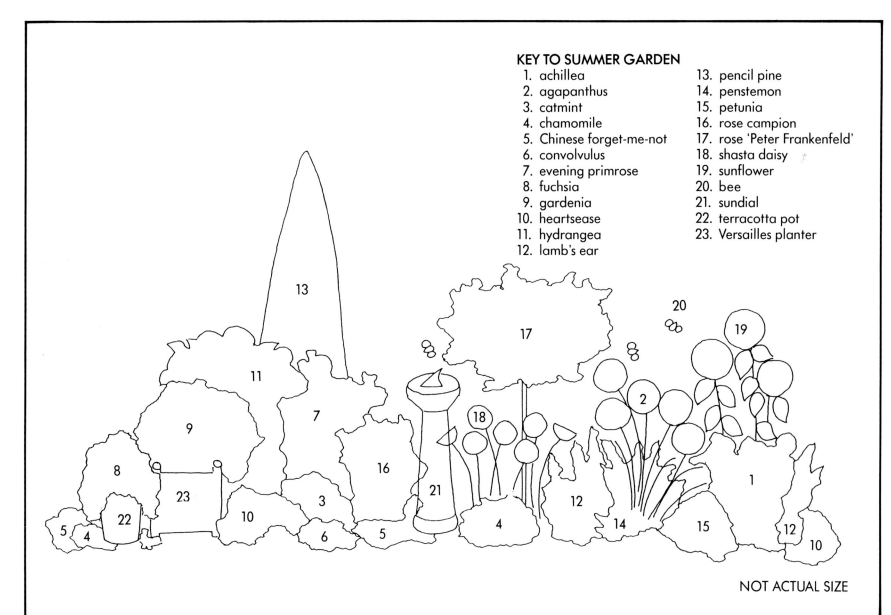

KEY TO SUMMER GARDEN
1. achillea
2. agapanthus
3. catmint
4. chamomile
5. Chinese forget-me-not
6. convolvulus
7. evening primrose
8. fuchsia
9. gardenia
10. heartsease
11. hydrangea
12. lamb's ear
13. pencil pine
14. penstemon
15. petunia
16. rose campion
17. rose 'Peter Frankenfeld'
18. shasta daisy
19. sunflower
20. bee
21. sundial
22. terracotta pot
23. Versailles planter

NOT ACTUAL SIZE

KEY TO 'KARDINAL' ROSE GARDEN

1. 'Kardinal rose
2. love-in-a-mist
3. pinks
4. primroses
5. ajuga
6. English daisies
7. Italian lavender
8. heartsease
9. coneflower

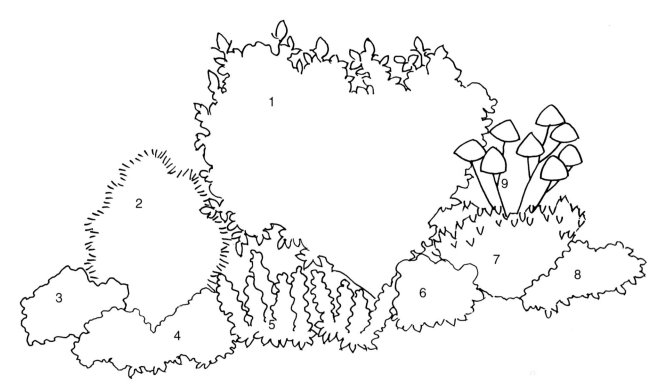

ACTUAL SIZE

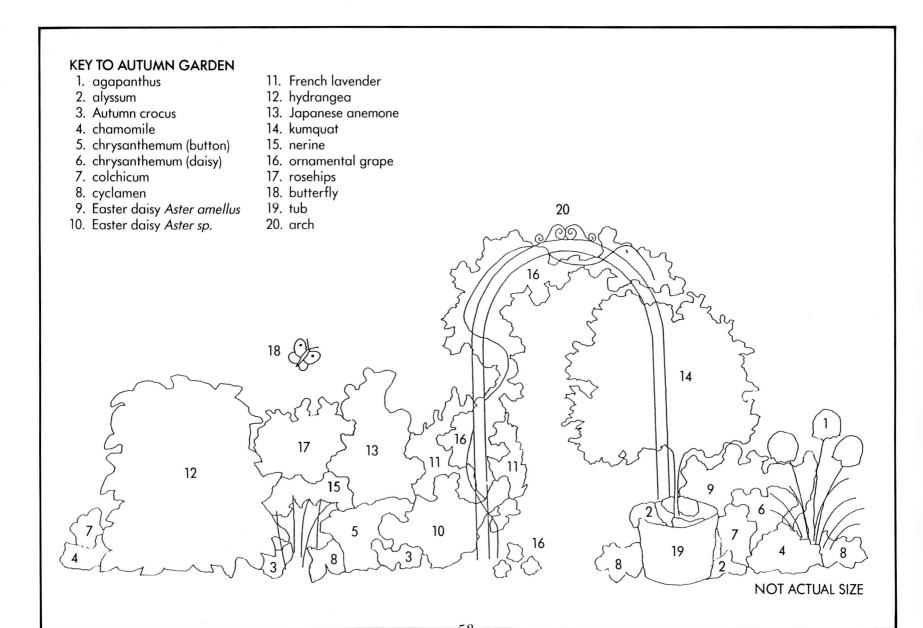

KEY TO AUTUMN GARDEN
1. agapanthus
2. alyssum
3. Autumn crocus
4. chamomile
5. chrysanthemum (button)
6. chrysanthemum (daisy)
7. colchicum
8. cyclamen
9. Easter daisy *Aster amellus*
10. Easter daisy *Aster sp.*
11. French lavender
12. hydrangea
13. Japanese anemone
14. kumquat
15. nerine
16. ornamental grape
17. rosehips
18. butterfly
19. tub
20. arch

NOT ACTUAL SIZE

KEY TO WINTER GARDEN

1. bergenia
2. cotoneaster horizontalis
3. Daphne
4. Diosma
5. garrya
6. jonquil (cream)
7. jonquil (yellow)
8. nandina
9. polyanthus (blue)
10. polyanthus (yellow)
11. primula
12. snowflake
13. violet
14. wallflower
15. silver birch
16. wattle
17. Winter iris
18. Winter rose (pink)
19. Winter rose (white)

NOT ACTUAL SIZE

CHAPTER 13

FLOWER GLOSSARY

This glossary gives the colour thread numbers and the method of working the individual flowers, trees, shrub, vines, garden ornaments and insects in this book. Also included are the needle type and the size you will need to use for each step.

Before commencing work, carefully read the details for each flower, relating the text to the drawing and the embroidered illustration. Remember the embroidered illustration will help you create the correct sense of scale.

DMC stranded thread has been used exclusively for the designs in this book. The threads have been carefully matched with the flowers and foliage for a realistic look. Many of the flowers come in other colours so you may like to experiment and match them to your own choice of threads.

Needles

Embroidery crewel needles are used for all stitches except bullion stitch, for which a straw or millinery needle is required.

Needles for the individual flowers vary in accordance with the stitch used and the number of strands required. Guidelines are as follows:

No 7 embroidery crewel needles for three to four strands of thread.

No 8 embroidery crewel needles for two strands of thread.

No 8 straw or millinery needles for two strands of thread.

No 9 embroidery crewel needles for one strand of thread.

No 9 straw or millinery needles for one strand of thread.

ACHILLEA 'CERISE QUEEN' *Achillea millefolium*

THREADS

ecru
602   cranberry — medium
3607   plum — light
3052   green grey — medium
3346   hunter green

STRANDS, STITCHES AND NEEDLES

stems		1 strand each 3052 and 3346 blended, couching, crewel 8
flowers	centres	2 strands ecru, French knots, crewel 8
	petals	1 strand each 602 and 3607 blended, French knots, crewel 8
leaves		1 strand each 3052 and 3346 blended, fly stitch, crewel 8

Work several stems in couching, branching at the top into three or four flower stalks. Stitch three or four French knots with ecru above the stalks for the centres of the flowers. Leave space for the petals. Work five French knots for the petals around each centre, forming a cluster of flowers. Work the leaves, starting at the tip and working back to the stem with small fly stitches.

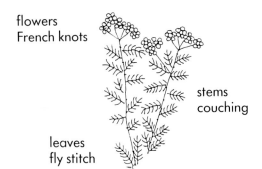

flowers
French knots

stems
couching

leaves
fly stitch

AGAPANTHUS *Agapanthus orientalis*

THREADS
340   blue violet — medium
341   blue violet — light
3346   hunter green

STRANDS, STITCHES AND NEEDLES

flowers	1 strand each 340 and 341 blended, fly stitch, crewel 8
stems	2 strands 3346, whipped stem stitch, crewel 8
leaves	2 strands 3346, stem stitch, crewel 8

Lightly mark the stems and arched leaves. Draw a circle at the top of each stem, leaving a small segment where the flower joins the stem. The flowers are worked in fly stitch with a small 'V' on the outside of the circle and the long tail going into the same hole in the centre. Work in a clockwise direction and stagger the length of the stitches. Add a few straight stitches in one strand of green radiating from the centre to depict the flowers' stalks.

The stems are worked in a single row of whipped stem stitch and the arched leaves in two rows of stem stitch, tapering to a point for the leaf's tip. Cross some leaves over the stems and over the other leaves to give a realistic effect. A bud can be added in satin stitch, if desired.

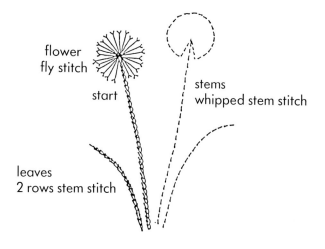

flower
fly stitch

start

stems
whipped stem stitch

leaves
2 rows stem stitch

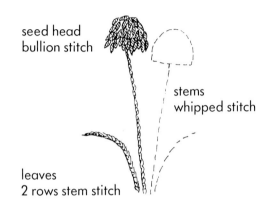

seed head
bullion stitch

stems
whipped stitch

leaves
2 rows stem stitch

leaves
straight stitch

flowers
French knots

AGAPANTHUS *Agapanthus orientalis* Autumn

THREADS
3347   yellow green — medium
3346   hunter green

STRANDS, STITCHES AND NEEDLES
seed heads   2 strands 3347, bullion stitch, straw 8
stems   2 strands 3347, whipped stem stitch, crewel 8
leaves   2 strands 3346, stem stitch, crewel 8

Mark stems, arched leaves and seed heads. The seed heads are worked first with bullion stitch (five wraps); start at the top and fill the marked area. The stems are worked with a single row of whipped stem stitch and the leaves with two rows of stem stitch, tapering to a point for the leaf's tip. Cross some leaves over the stems and over the other leaves to give a realistic effect.

ALYSSUM (SWEET ALICE) *Lobularia maritima*

THREADS
553   violet
3051   green grey — dark

STRANDS, STITCHES AND NEEDLES
flowers   1 strand 553, French knots, crewel 9
leaves   1 strand 3051, straight stitch, crewel 9

Flowers are worked in clusters of six to eight French knots. Add small, straight stitches around the edge of the flowers for the leaves. Alyssum is useful for filling in spaces between other flowers.

AUTUMN CROCUS *Sternbergia lutea*

THREADS
973   canary — bright
3346   hunter green

STRANDS, STITCHES AND NEEDLES
flowers   2 strands 973, lazy daisy stitch, crewel 8
stems and leaves   2 strands 3346, straight stitch, crewel 8

The crocus flowers are very small; work them first with three lazy daisy stitches, slightly overlapping and pointing upwards. The stems and leaves are added below the flowers with straight stitches.

flowers
lazy daisy stitch

stems & leaves
straight stitch

BERGENIA *Bergenia cordifolia*

THREADS
3609   plum — ultra light
3064   sportsman flesh — very dark
3328   salmon — dark
3346   hunter green

STRANDS, STITCHES AND NEEDLES

leaves		2 strands 3346, buttonhole stitch, crewel 8
stems		1 strand each 3064 and 3328 blended, stem stitch, crewel 8
flowers	centres	1 strand each 3064 and 3328 blended, French knots, crewel 8
	petals	3 strands 3609, French knots, crewel 8

Draw three or four paddle-shaped leaves with a central vein. Work the leaves in buttonhole stitch starting at the base and working around the leaf and, at the same time, to a point two-thirds of the way along the central vein. Work two or three stems in stem stitch, working upwards from the leaves. With the same thread, above each stem, stitch five or six French knots approximately 3 mm (⅛″) apart for the centres of the flowers. Work five French knots for the petals around each centre, forming a cluster of flowers.

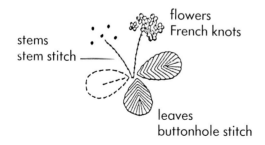

stems
stem stitch

flowers
French knots

leaves
buttonhole stitch

BUGLEWEED or BLUE BUGLE *Ajuga reptans* 'Purpurea'

THREADS

327	violet very dark
333	blue violet very dark
3041	antique violet medium
3051	green grey dark

STRANDS, STITCHES AND NEEDLES

stems	2 strands 3041, stem stitch, crewel 8
leaves	1 strand each 327 and 3051 blended, chain stalks, crewel 9
flowers	2 strands 333, French knots, crewel 8

flowers
French knots

stems
stem stitch

leaves
chain stalk

Draw short straight stems for the flower spikes and work them in stem stitch. Work the leaves on the stems (in pairs) with small chain stalks and with a tiny one at the top. Work rosettes of larger leaves on the 'ground' coming back to the stems.

A chain stalk is a lazy daisy stitch worked with an extended anchoring stitch. Ajuga leaves are worked in the opposite direction to lazy daisy stitch, ie back towards the stem.

Add the flowers to the flower spikes with French knots, one in the axil of each leaf.

 chain stalk

CATMINT *Nepeta cataria*

THREADS
209   lavender — dark
368   pistachio green — light

STRANDS, STITCHES AND NEEDLES
foliage   2 strands 368, fly stitch, crewel 8
flowers   2 strands 209, French knots, crewel 8

Work the foliage with fly stitch, starting at the top of the stems and working back to the base. Overlap some stems until a well-shaped, small bush is formed. The flowers are added with French knots on the top of the stems and on either side to halfway down the stems.

flowers
French knots

foliage
fly stitch

CHAMOMILE *Anthemis tinctoria*

THREADS
444   lemon — dark
783   topaz — medium
3363   pine green — medium

STRANDS, STITCHES AND NEEDLES
foliage   1 strand 3363, fly stitch, crewel 9
flowers   petals   1 strand 444, lazy daisy stitch, crewel 9
                   centres   2 strands 783, French knot, crewel 8

Work the foliage with fly stitch, starting at the top of the stems and working back to the base. Overlap some stems until a well-shaped, small bush is formed. Work small daisies at the top of the stems and scatter more over the foliage. These are worked with eight to ten lazy daisy stitches for the petals, leaving a space for the centre. Work some half flowers to depict a side-on view. Add the flower centres with a French knot.

flowers
lazy daisy stitch
centre French knots

foliage
fly stitch

CHINESE FORGET-ME-NOT *Cynoglossum amabile*

THREADS

793   cornflower blue — medium
333   blue violet — very dark
3052   green grey — medium

STRANDS, STITCHES AND NEEDLES

flowers   centre   2 strands 333, French knots, crewel 8
           petals   2 strands 793, French knots, crewel 8
leaves   2 strands 3052, lazy daisy stitch, crewel 8

Work centres first with one French knot and surround very closely with five French knots for the petals. Scatter lazy daisy stitch leaves underneath the flowers.

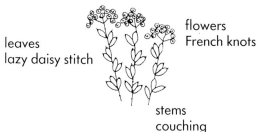

leaves
lazy daisy stitch

flowers
French knots

CHRYSANTHEMUM (BUTTON) *Chrysanthemum morifolium*

THREADS

307   lemon
3362   pine green — dark

STRANDS, STITCHES AND NEEDLES

stems   2 strands 3362, couching, crewel 8 with 1 strand crewel 9
leaves   2 strands 3362, lazy daisy stitch, crewel 8
flowers   3 strands 307, French knots, crewel 7

Mark required number of stems and work them in couching. Using the one strand of couching thread, work three or four small branches at the top of each stem. The leaves splay upwards from the stems and are formed by working two or three lazy daisy stitches together. Add the flowers at the top of the stems with French knots.

leaves
lazy daisy stitch

flowers
French knots

stems
couching

CHRYSANTHEMUM (DAISY) *Chrysanthemum morifolium*

THREADS

356   terracotta — medium
758   terracotta — very light
725   topaz
3362 pine green — dark

STRANDS, STITCHES AND NEEDLES

stems		2 strands 3362, couching, crewel 8 with 1 strand, crewel 9
leaves		2 strands 3362, lazy daisy stitch, crewel 8
flowers	petals	1 strand each 356 and 758 blended, straight stitch, crewel 8
	centre	2 strands 725, French knots, crewel 8

Mark required number of stems and work them in couching. The leaves splay upwards from the stems and are formed by working two or three lazy daisy stitches together. Mark the flowers at the top of the stems with a circle and with a smaller centre circle. Work the petals first with straight stitches of varying lengths. Add the centre with three French knots. A half flower adds interest.

flowers
straight stitch
centre French knots

stems
couching

leaves
lazy daisy stitch

COLCHICUM *Colchicum autumnale*

THREADS
ecru
554   violet — light
211   lavender — light
772   yellow green — very light
3013   khaki green — light

STRANDS, STITCHES AND NEEDLES
flowers   1 strand each ecru, 554 and 211 blended, lazy
                     daisy stitch, crewel 7
stems   1 strand each ecru, 772 and 3013 blended, crewel
                     7, couching 1 strand 3013, crewel 9

Lightly mark the stems and work in couching. Leave enough space for
the flowers; they are placed above the stems. Work the flowers with
three lazy daisy stitches overlapping slightly from the top of the stem
and pointing upwards.

flowers
lazy daisy stitch

stems
couching

CONEFLOWER *Echinacea purpurea*

THREADS
316   antique mauve – medium
400   mahogany – dark
469   avocado green
3722 shell pink – medium
3726 antique mauve – dark

STRANDS, STITCHES AND NEEDLES
stems   2 strands 3722, stem stitch, crewel 8
flowers
  petals   2 strands 3726, lazy daisy stitch, crewel 8
  faded petals 2 strands 316, lazy daisy stitch, crewel 8
centre (cone) 2 strands 400, French knots, crewel 8
leaves   2 strands 469, double lazy daisy, lazy daisy stitch and
                 straight stitch, crewel 8

Draw the stems and work them in stem stitch.
Draw cone shapes for the flowers. Work the petals with lazy daisy stitch.
Use 316 for the more mature, faded and drooping petals and 3726 for
the newer flowers.
Fill in the cones with French knots.
Work the leaves in pairs with double lazy daisy stitch and attach to stem
with a straight stitch stalk. Add smaller axillary leaves with lazy daisy
stitch.

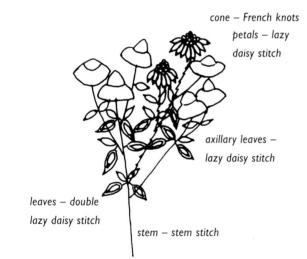

cone – French knots
petals – lazy daisy stitch
axillary leaves – lazy daisy stitch
leaves – double lazy daisy stitch
stem – stem stitch

CONVOLVULUS *Convolvulus mauretanicus*

THREADS
210   lavender — medium
320   pistachio green — medium

STRANDS, STITCHES AND NEEDLES
flowers   1 strand 210, buttonhole stitch, crewel 9
leaves   2 strands 320, lazy daisy stitch, crewel 8

Work the flowers with very small circles of buttonhole stitch. Add lazy daisy leaves underneath and between the flowers.

flowers
buttonhole stitch

leaves
lazy daisy stitch

COTONEASTER *horizontalis*

THREADS
347   salmon — very dark
937   avocado green — medium
840   beige brown — medium

STRANDS, STITCHES AND NEEDLES
branches   2 strands 840, stem stitch, crewel 8
leaves   2 strands 939, lazy daisy stitch, crewel 8
berries   2 strands 347, French knots, crewel 8

Work the branches in stem stitch. Add the leaves with tiny lazy daisy stitches alternating down the branches, then add the berries with French knots between the leaves.

berries
French knots

leaves
lazy daisy stitch

branches
stem stitch

COTTAGE PINKS *Dianthus plumarius*

THREADS
blanc neige
819   baby pink – light
503   blue green – medium

STRANDS AND STITCHES USED

stems	2 strands 503, stem stitch, crewel 8
leaves	2 strands 503, straight stitch, crewel8
flowers	1 strand each blanc neige and 819 blended, straight stitch crewel 9
buds	1 strand 819, bullion stitch, straw 9

flowers
straight stitch

stems
stem stitch

buds
bullion stitch

leaves
straight stitch

Lightly mark and work in stem stitch. Work leaves in straight stitch at base of plant and on the stems. Flowers are worked in straight stitch (not too many), working from the outside into the same hole in the centre. Vary the length of the stitches to give a realistic look. Buds are worked in bullion stitch of nine wraps and are scattered throughout the foliage.

CYCLAMEN *Cyclamen hederifolium*

THREADS
3609   plum — ultra light
501   blue green — dark
503   blue green — medium

STRANDS, STITCHES AND NEEDLES

leaves	1 strand each 501 and 503 blended, buttonhole stitch, crewel 8
flowers	2 strands 3609, lazy daisy stitch, crewel 8
stems	1 strand 501, stem stich, crewel 9

First work clusters of heart-shaped leaves in buttonhole stitch. Work flowers above the leaves using two or three lazy daisy stitches overlapping them slightly from the same point and pointing them upwards or fanning to the side. Work stems in stem stitch offset slightly from the centre of the flower. Check illustration for position.

flowers
lazy daisy stitch

stems
stem stitch

leaves
buttonhole stitch

CYCLAMEN *Cyclamen sp.*

Note: There are two colours for this flower

THREADS
Blanc neige
or
335   rose

501   blue green – dark
503   blue green – medium

STRANDS AND STITCHES USED

leaves	1 strand each 501 and 503 blended, buttonhole stitch, crewel 8
flowers	2 strands blanc neige or 335, lazy daisy stitch, crewel 8
stems	1 strand 501, stem stitch, crewel 9

First work clusters of heart-shaped leaves in buttonhole stitch. Work flowers above the leaves using two or three lazy daisy stitches overlapping slightly from the same point and pointing upwards or fanning to the side. Work stems in stem stitch offset slightly from the centre of the flower. Check illustration for position.

flowers
lazy daisy stitch

stems
stem stitch

leaves
buttonhole stitch

DAFFODIL *Narcissus sp.*

THREADS

743	yellow – medium
745	yellow – light pale
372	mustard – light
3363	pine green – medium

STRANDS, STITCHES AND NEEDLES

stem and leaves	2 strands 3363, stem stitch, crewel 8
flowers trumpet	2 strands 743, buttonhole stitch, crewel 8
petals	2 strands 745, lazy daisy stitch, crewel 8
bracts	2 strands 372, lazy daisy stitch, crewel 8

Lightly mark stems and leaves and work in stem stitch. The aura of realism can be enhanced by working some leaves so that they bend at an angle. Work the trumpet of the daffodil using three buttonhole stitches commencing from the left-hand side of the outside edge. Place two or three lazy daisy stitch petals at the top of the trumpet. Work one lazy daisy stitch for the bract to attach flower to stem.

bract
lazy daisy stitch

flowers
trumpet – buttonhole stitch
petals – lazy daisy stitch

stems and leaves
stem stitch

DAPHNE *Daphne odora*

THREADS
blanc neige
316   antique mauve — medium
611   drab brown — dark
987   forest green — dark

STRANDS, STITCHES AND NEEDLES

flowers	1 strand each blanc neige and 316 blended, French knots, crewel 8
leaves	2 strands 987, lazy daisy stitch, crewel 8
branches	2 strands 611, long bullion stitch, straw 8

Mark trunk and branches of the Daphne. Some flowers are worked before placement of branches and others after, so a few of the leaves can overlap the branches to create a more realistic-looking shrub. Work flowers in clusters of seven to ten French knots, surrounded by approximately seven to ten lazy daisy leaves. The number of wraps for the bullion stitch branches will vary depending on the length required. Work on the basis that an average of ten wraps measures approximately 6 mm (¼″), and 50 wraps approximately 33 mm (1¼″). The long bullion stitch branches are couched into position.

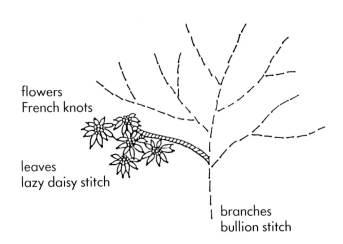

flowers
French knots

leaves
lazy daisy stitch

branches
bullion stitch

DELPHINIUM *Delphinium elatum*

Each flower is worked in a different shade of blue. To give a sense of perspective, place the palest shade of flower in the background and the darkest shade in the foreground.

THREADS
792   cornflower blue – dark
793   cornflower blue – medium
794   cornflower blue – light
987   forest green – dark

STRANDS, STITCHES AND NEEDLES
buds   3 strands 987, French knots, crewel 7
           2 strands blue and 1 strands 987 blended, French knots, crewel 7
flowers   3 strands and 4 strands 792, French knots, crewel 7. or
           3 strands and 4 strands 793, French knots, crewel 7. or
           3 strands and 4 strands 794, French knots, crewel 7
leaves   2 strands 987, lazy daisy stitch, crewel 8

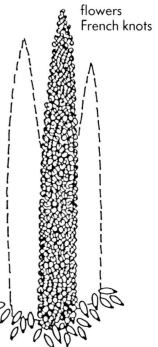

flowers
French knots

leaves
lazy daisy stitch

The use of a small embroidery hoop when working these flowers will make your task far quicker and easier. Mark three conical shapes for working down with three strands of green, then two strands of the chosen blue blended with one strand of green. Graduate to three strands of blue. Do not finish in a straight line but blend each new thread combination. Continue down the flower changing to four strands of blue towards the base. Place lazy daisy leaves around the base of the flowers, if necessary or desired. As these flowers grow very tall and are time consuming to work, they are ideal for placing behind other flowers.

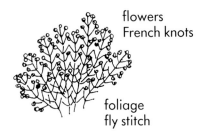

flowers
French knots

foliage
fly stitch

DIOSMA *Coleonema pulchrum*

THREADS
605   cranberry — very light
470   avocado green — light

STRANDS, STITCHES AND NEEDLES
foliage   2 strands 470, fly stitch, crewel 8
flowers   2 strands 605, French knots, crewel 8

Lightly mark the outline of the area for the foliage and work in fly stitch. Flowers are worked in clusters of French knots at the top of the foliage, with more scattered throughout.

DUTCH HYACINTH *Hyacinthus orientalis*

THREADS
963   dusty rose – very light
3689   mauve – light
3347   yellow green – medium

flowers
French knots

stems and leaves
straight stitch

STRANDS, STITCHES AND NEEDLES
stem and leaves   3 strands 3347, straight stitch, crewel 7
flowers   2 strands 963 and 1 strand 3689 blended, French
                     knots, crewel 7

Sew one long straight stitch as stem with two shorter straight stitches either side as leaves. Work French knots closely down either side and over the stem to form a rectangular shape.

EASTER DAISY (MICHAELMAS) *Aster amellus*

THREADS

210   lavender — medium
444   lemon — dark
937   avocado green — medium

STRANDS, STITCHES AND NEEDLES

stems	2 strands 937, couching, crewel 8 with 1 strand, crewel 9
leaves	2 strands 937, lazy daisy stitch, crewel 8
flowers	1 strand 210, straight stitch, crewel 9
centre	1 strand 444, French knot, crewel 9

flowers
straight stitch
centre French knot

stems
couching

leaves
lazy daisy stitch

This Easter or Michaelmas daisy grows 60 cm (2′) high. Mark required number of stems and work them in couching. Add the lazy daisy leaves, alternating them down each side of the stems. The very small daisies are placed at the top of the stem and down each side, between and over the leaves. Work the daisies in straight stitch from the outside into the same hole in the centre. Vary the length of the stitches to give a realistic look. Add the centres with a French knot.

EASTER DAISY (MICHAELMAS) *Aster sp.*

THREADS
552   violet — medium
726   topaz — light
3346   hunter green

STRANDS, STITCHES AND NEEDLES

stems		2 strands 3346, couching, crewel 8 with 1 strand, crewel 9
leaves		2 strands 3346, lazy daisy stitch, crewel 8
flowers		1 strand 552, straight stitch, crewel 9
	centre	2 strands 726, French knot, crewel 8

These Easter or Michaelmas daisies are not as tall as *Aster amellus*. The flowers are larger and deeper in colour. Mark the stems and work them in couching. Add the lazy daisy leaves, alternating them down each side of the stem. The daisies are placed in clusters at the top of each stem. Work the daisies in straight stitch from the outside into the same hole in the centre. Vary the length of the stitches to give a realistic look. Add the centres with a French knot.

flowers
straight stitch
centre French knot

stems
couching

leaves
lazy daisy stitch

ENGLISH BLUEBELL *Endymion nonscripta*
(previously *Scilla nonscripta*)

THREADS
341   blue-violet – light
3346   hunter green

STRANDS, STITCHES AND NEEDLES
flowers   2 strands 341, buttonhole stitch, crewel 8
stems   2 strands 3346, couching, crewel 8
leaves   2 strands 3346, stem stitch, crewel 8

Lightly draw in stems; leave a generous space between stems (the flowers take up more space than you might at first think). Stems are worked in couching. Work flowers from the bottom in alternate bells of two buttonhole stitches on either side of the stem. Just one bell is worked on the top of the flower to form a point. Add leaves in stem stitch.

stems
couching

flowers
buttonhole stitch

leaves
stem stitch

ENGLISH DAISIES *Bellis perennis*

THREADS
blanc neige
223	shell pink – light
224	shell pink – very light
444	lemon – dark
471	avocado green – very light
3346	hunter green

STRANDS, STITCHES AND NEEDLES

flowers	petals	1 strand each 223 and blanc neige blended, straight stitch, crewel 8
		1 strand each 224 and blanc neige blended, straight stitch, crewel 8
	centre	2 strands 444, French knot
stems		2 strands 471, couching, crewel 8
leaves		2 strands 3346, lazy daisy stitch, crewel 8

petals –
straight stitch

centre –
French knot

stems –
couching

leaves – lazy
daisy stitch

Draw small circles for the flowers with a dot for the centre.
Work petals with straight stitches from the outside circle down into the centre (leave space for centre). Work petals in quarters first and fill in between these with two or three more petals. Add in French knot centres.
Add short stems from the flowers with couching.
Work the leaves with lazy daisy stitches at the base of the stems.

ENGLISH PRIMROSE *Primula vulgaris*

THREADS

745	yellow – light pale
612	drab brown – medium
471	avocado green – very light

STRANDS, STITCHES AND NEEDLES

flowers	petals	2 strands 745, lazy daisy stitch, crewel 8
	centre	2 strands 612, French knot, crewel 8
stems		2 strands 471, stem stitch or couching, crewel 8
leaves		2 strands 471, lazy daisy stitch, crewel 8

Work flowers with five petals in lazy daisy stitch radiating from the centre. Some flowers may only have four petals in the centre of each flower. Work stems in stem stitch or couching and sew lazy daisy leaves randomly around the base.

stems
couching

flowers
lazy daisy stitch

centre
French knot

leaves
lazy daisy stitch

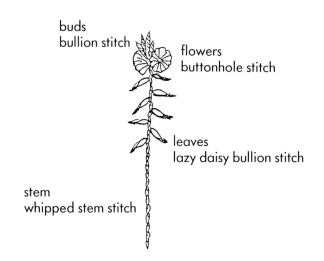

buds
bullion stitch

flowers
buttonhole stitch

leaves
lazy daisy bullion stitch

stem
whipped stem stitch

EVENING PRIMROSE *Oenothera laciniata nocturna*

THREADS
445   lemon — light
356   terracotta — medium
3347   yellow green — medium

STRANDS, STITCHES AND NEEDLES

buds	1 strand each 356 and 3347 blended, bullion stitch, straw 8
stems	1 strand each 356 and 3347 blended, whipped stem stitch, crewel 8
flowers	2 strands 445, buttonhole stitch, crewel 8
leaves	2 strands 3347, lazy daisy bullion stitch (4 wraps), straw 8

Mark required number of stems on your fabric and work them with whipped stem stitch. The buds are worked at the top of each stem with three or four bullion stitches (nine wraps). The flowers are placed just below the buds attached to the stem. Full flowers are formed with a circle of buttonhole stitch and side-on flowers with a part circle of buttonhole stitch. The leaves are worked with lazy daisy bullion stitch (four wraps) down either side of the stems, alternating at intervals.

FLOWERING ALMOND CHERRY (PRUNUS)
Prunus glandulosa 'Rosa'

THREADS

3689	mauve – light
605	cranberry – very light
610	drab brown – very dark
988	forest green – medium

STRANDS, STITCHES AND NEEDLES

branches	2 strands 610, couching, crewel 8
minor branches	1 strand 610, straight stitch, crewel 9
flowers	2 strands 605 and 1 strand 3689 blended, French knots, crewel 7
leaves	1 strand 988, straight stitch, crewel 9

Lightly draw in branches and couch. Add minor branches in straight stitch. Cover heavily with French knot flowers and place leaves throughout in small straight stitches.

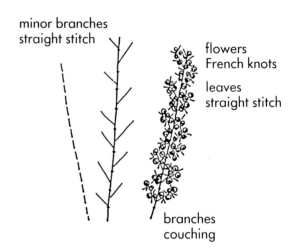

minor branches
straight stitch

flowers
French knots

leaves
straight stitch

branches
couching

FORGET-ME-NOT *Myosotis sylvatica*

There is a choice of three colours for these flowers.

THREADS
800   delft – pale
or
3354   dusty rose – light
or
809   delft

726   topaz – light
989   forest green

STRANDS, STITCHES AND NEEDLES

flowers	centre	2 strands 726, French knots, crewel 8
	petals	2 strands 800 or 3354 or 809, French knots, crewel 8
leaves		2 strands 989, lazy daisy stitch, crewel 8

Work centres first in one French knot and surround very closely with five French knots for petals. Scatter lazy daisy stitch leaves sparingly underneath the flowers.

flowers
French knots

leaves
lazy daisy stitch

FORSYTHIA *Forsythia suspensa*

THREADS

726   topaz – light
372   mustard – light
730   olive green – very dark

STRANDS, STITCHES AND NEEDLES
branches   2 strands 372, stem stitch, crewel 8
leaves   2 strands 730, lazy daisy stitch, crewel 8
flowers   2 strands 726, small straight stitch, crewel 8

Lightly draw in branches and work in stem stitch. Work two or three leaves in lazy daisy stitch from the top of the branches, pointing upwards. Flowers are worked in two or three small straight stitches either side of, and over, the branches, approximately every 5mm (⅛") and angled out and downwards.

Forsythia designed by Tineke Mitter.

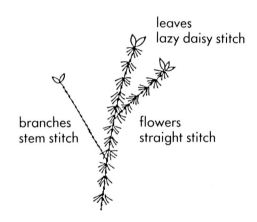

leaves
lazy daisy stitch

branches
stem stitch

flowers
straight stitch

FOXGLOVE *Digitalis purpurea*

Threads
225   shell pink – very light
224   shell pink – light
223   shell pink – medium
3363   pine green – medium

STRANDS, STITCHES AND NEEDLES
stems   2 strands 3363, stem stitch or couching, crewel 8
buds   2 strands 3363, French knots, crewel 8
         1 strand 3363 and 225 blended, French knot 2 twists, crewel 8
flowers 2 strands 225, 2 buttonhole stitches, crewel 8
         1 strands 225 and 224 blended, 3 buttonhole stitches, crewel 8
         2 strands 224, 3 buttonhole stitches, crewel 8
         1 strand 224 and 223 blended, 3 buttonhole stitches, crewel 8
         2 strands 223, 3 buttonhole stitches (if required or desired), crewel 8
leaves   2 strands 3363, satin stitch, crewel 8

Mark stems and work in couching or stem stitch, starting at the base. With the same thread, at the top of the stem work three or four buds in French knots. Finish off. Do not extend thread across to the next stem: the green thread will show through your work. Stitch four or five buds in the blended threads in French knots (two twists).

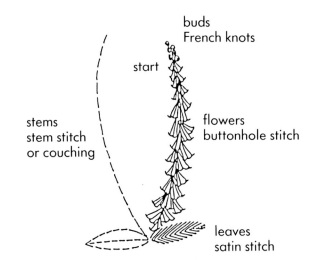

buds
French knots

start

stems
stem stitch
or couching

flowers
buttonhole stitch

leaves
satin stitch

The flowers are worked from the top of the stem, graduating in colour as listed above. Work five or six trumpets in each thread combination. Before commencing, please check where to start on flower illustration. Work trumpets form left to right, placing on either side of the stem, crossing over stems and staggering them as you work down. Add an extra trumpet to the side and centre here and there. They should be slightly longer and placed more thickly at the base of the stem.

Draw elongated leaves with a central vein. Stitch outline in one strand of green in small running stitch. Work leaf in satin stitch: use very slanting stitches and, starting at leaf base, work along one side of leaf, straightening stitches to form a point. Then work back down the other side. For those who don't like satin stitch, these leaves can be worked in an elongated satin leaf stitch. Foxgloves can also be worked behind other flowers; the inclusion of leaves is then unnecessary.

FRENCH LAVENDER *Lavandula dentata*

THREADS
208   lavender — very dark
3053   green grey

STRANDS, STITCHES AND NEEDLES
foliage   2 strands 3053, fly stitch, crewel 8
flower heads   1 strand each 208 and 3053 blended, bullion
                              stitch, straw 8

Lightly mark the branches for the foliage. Work each branch starting at the top with a straight stitch and work down in fly stitch to the base. Overlap some branches and stitch some smaller branches for a realistic-looking lavender bush.

Work flower heads, following the angle of the stem, in bullion stitch (nine wraps) at the top of each branch. Scatter more throughout the foliage. To stitch a pointed lavender head, take the needle out a little further when anchoring the bullion stitch.

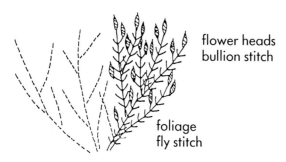

flower heads
bullion stitch

foliage
fly stitch

FUCHSIA *Fuchsia sp.*

THREADS
327   violet — very dark
309   rose — deep
315   antique mauve — very dark
470   avocado green — light

STRANDS, STITCHES AND NEEDLES
flower	trumpet	2 strands 327, buttonhole stitch, crewel 8
	petals	2 strands 309, lazy daisy bullion stitch, and lazy daisy stitch, straw 8
	stamens	1 strand 315, French knot stalk, crewel 9
	calyx	2 strands 470, French knot, 2 twists, crewel 8
stems		2 strands 470, stem stitch, crewel 8
leaves		2 strands 470, lazy daisy stitch, crewel 8

Note: Use a small hoop for good tension when working French knot stalks.

trumpet
buttonhole stitch

petals
lazy daisy bullion stitch
lazy daisy stitch

stamens
French knot stalks

leaves
lazy daisy stitch

The trumpet of the fuchsia is worked first with three buttonhole stitches commencing from the left-hand side of the outside edge. Place three lazy daisy bullion stitches with one wrap, starting above the trumpet, forming the petals. Finish them over the trumpet and on either side of it. To complete the petals, work a small lazy daisy stitch pointing upward from the top of the petals. Add three stamens, coming from below the trumpet, with French knot stalks.

For the calyx, work a French knot with two twists above the flower. Stems are then worked with stem stitch where required, and leaves in lazy daisy stitch are scattered at random.

stem
stem stitch

flowers

 outer petals
buttonhole stitch

 centre
bullion stitch

 leaves
lazy daisy stitch

bud
bullion stitch
calyx — fly stitch

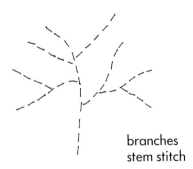 branches
stem stitch

GARDENIA 'Florida' *Gardenia augusta*

THREADS
blanc neige
3347   yellow green — medium
3346   hunter green
611   drab brown — dark

STRANDS, STITCHES AND NEEDLES

branches	2 strands 611, stem stitch, crewel 8
flowers	2 strands blanc neige, buttonhole stitch, crewel 8 and bullion stitch (5, 6 and 7 wraps), straw 8
buds	2 strands blanc neige, bullion stitch (7 wraps), straw 8
	2 strands 3347, bullion stitch (7 wraps), crewel 8
calyx	2 strands 3347, fly stitch and straight stitch, crewel 8
leaves	2 strands 3347, lazy daisy stitch, crewel 8
	2 strands 3346, lazy daisy stitch, crewel 8

Pencil in the branches and work in stem stitch. Mark the flower shapes as illustrated on the bush. Work around the outside of the flowers with buttonhole stitch, leaving the centre clear of stitches. Build up the centre of the flower in the same way as a 'grub rose' using bullion stitch. First, work two bullions with five wraps for the centre. Then, work three bullions with six wraps around, and finally two or three bullions with seven wraps until a well-formed flower is completed. The number of bullions required for the centre will depend on the size of your flower.

The buds are worked with two seven-wrap bullion stitches side by side. Add a calyx with a fly stitch around the bud and a straight stitch into the centre of the bud. The leaves are worked in lazy daisy stitch with the two greens.

French Lavender

Grape Hyacinth

Gypsophila

Heartsease

Lily-of-the-valley

Magnolia

Periwinkle

Rose

Shasta Daisy

Snowflake

Solomon's Seal

Violet

Hollyhock

Winter Rose

Wisteria

FLOWER SAMPLER

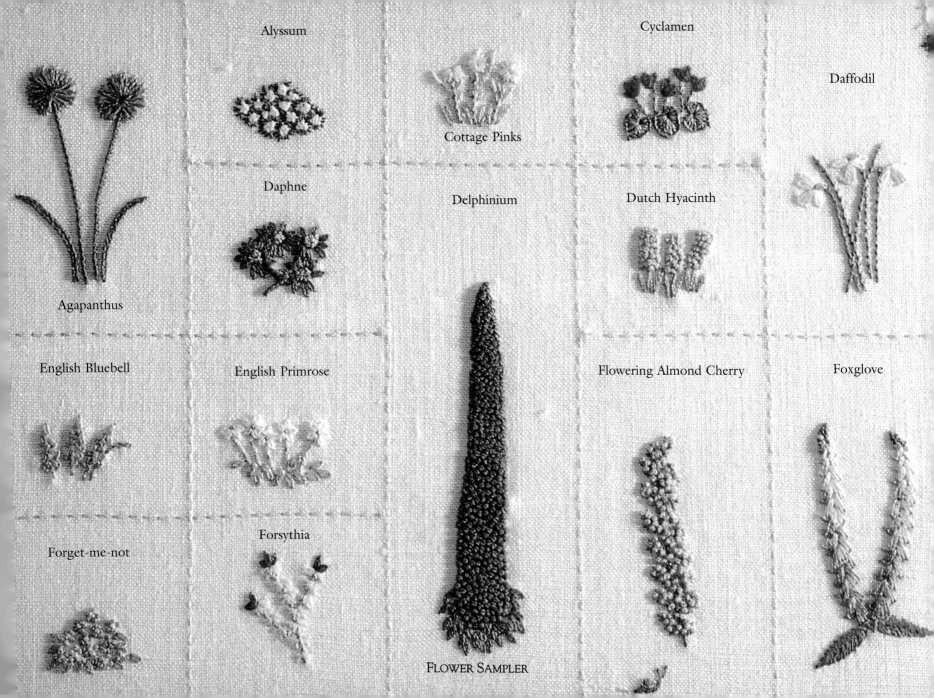

Alyssum

Cyclamen

Daffodil

Cottage Pinks

Daphne

Delphinium

Dutch Hyacinth

Agapanthus

English Bluebell

English Primrose

Flowering Almond Cherry

Foxglove

Forget-me-not

Forsythia

FLOWER SAMPLER

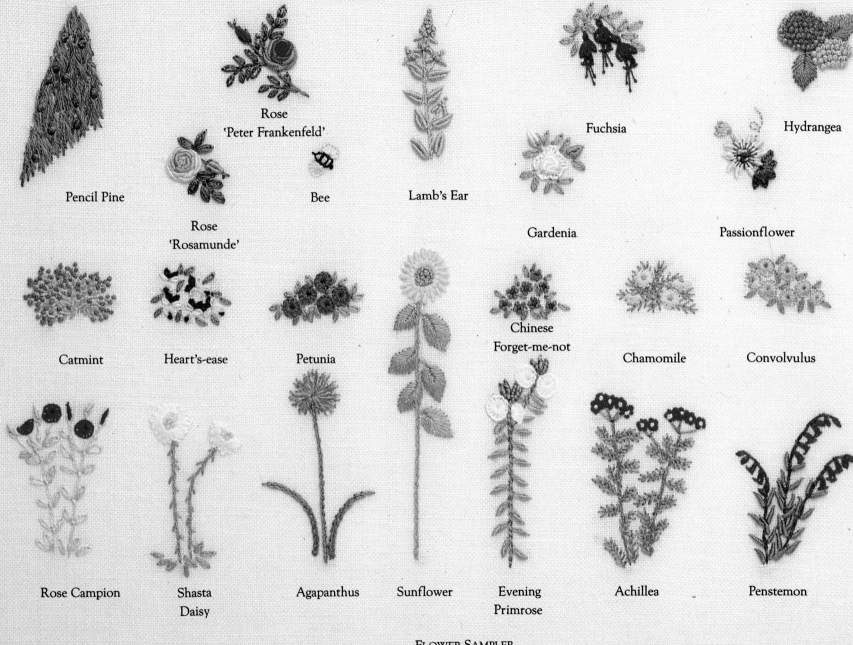

Pencil Pine

Rose
'Peter Frankenfeld'

Rose
'Rosamunde'

Bee

Lamb's Ear

Fuchsia

Gardenia

Hydrangea

Passionflower

Catmint

Heart's-ease

Petunia

Chinese
Forget-me-not

Chamomile

Convolvulus

Rose Campion

Shasta
Daisy

Agapanthus

Sunflower

Evening
Primrose

Achillea

Penstemon

FLOWER SAMPLER

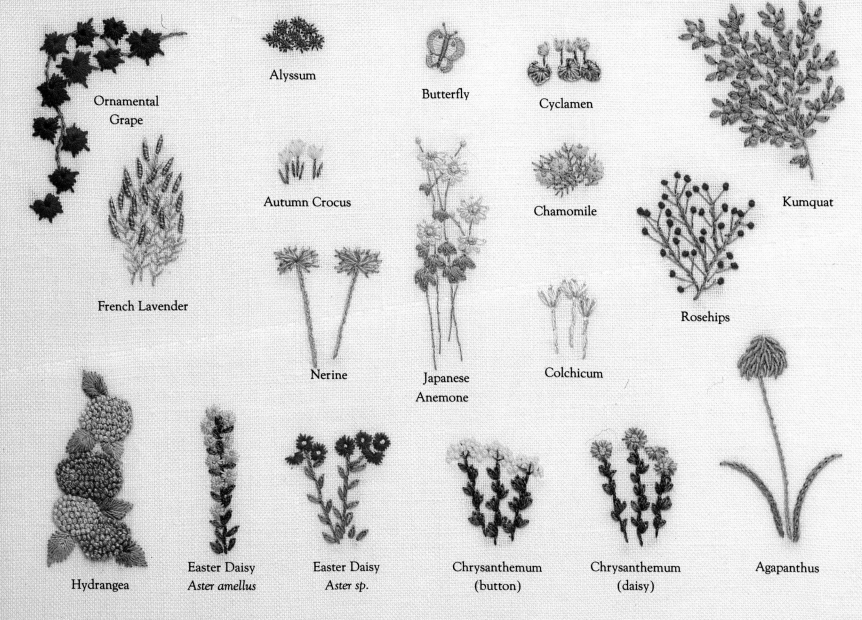

Ornamental
Grape

Alyssum

Butterfly

Cyclamen

Kumquat

French Lavender

Autumn Crocus

Chamomile

Rosehips

Nerine

Japanese
Anemone

Colchicum

Hydrangea

Easter Daisy
Aster amellus

Easter Daisy
Aster sp.

Chrysanthemum
(button)

Chrysanthemum
(daisy)

Agapanthus

FLOWER SAMPLER

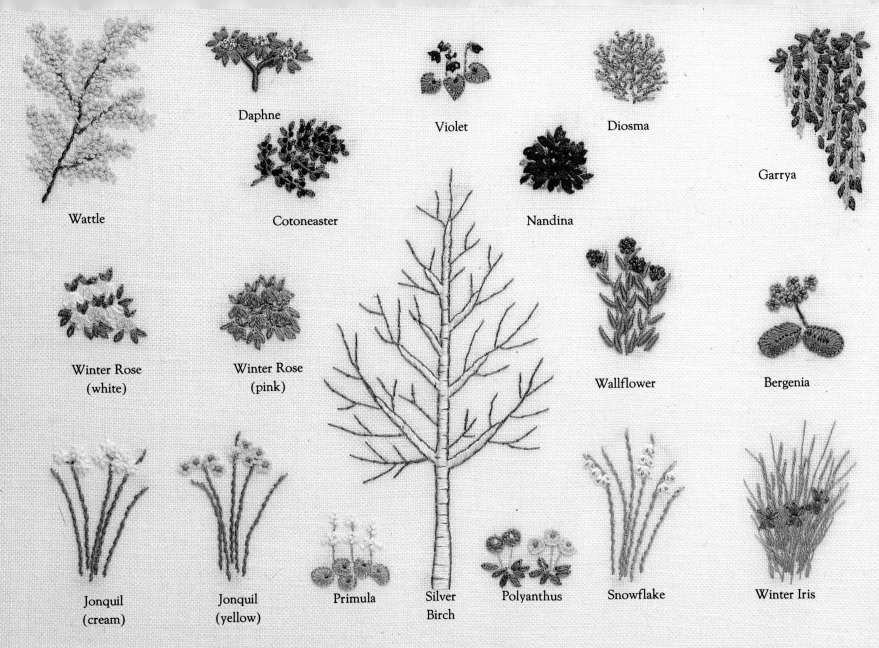

Daphne

Violet

Diosma

Wattle

Cotoneaster

Nandina

Garrya

Winter Rose
(white)

Winter Rose
(pink)

Wallflower

Bergenia

Jonquil
(cream)

Jonquil
(yellow)

Primula

Silver
Birch

Polyanthus

Snowflake

Winter Iris

FLOWER SAMPLER

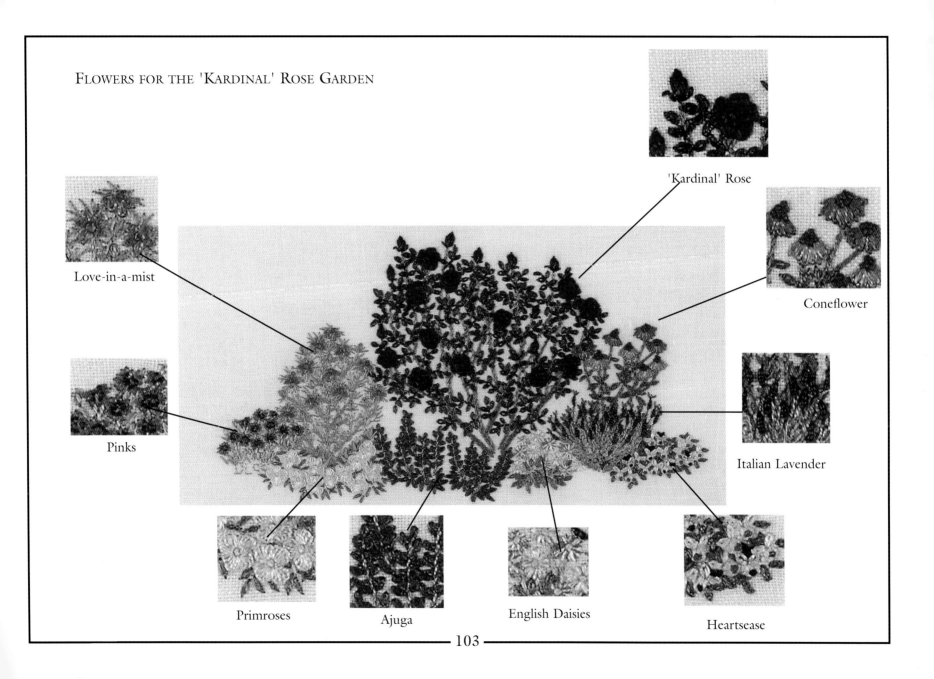

FLOWERS FOR THE 'KARDINAL' ROSE GARDEN

'Kardinal' Rose

Love-in-a-mist

Coneflower

Pinks

Italian Lavender

Primroses

Ajuga

English Daisies

Heartsease

SUMMER GARLAND

105

GIFT IDEAS

106

Key to Embroidered Gifts

1 Pincushion by Lois Kinsman
2 Pincushion by Chris Bromfield
3 Sewing baskets by Jane Fisk
4 Embroidered pullover by Diana Lampe
5 Cushion by Jane Fisk
6 Cushion by Maggie Taylor
7 Coathanger by Diana Lampe
8 Wickerwork basket by Jane Fisk
9 Lavender sachet by Jane Fisk
10 Towel by Jane Fisk
11 Brooch by Diana Lampe
12 Handkerchiefs by Jane Fisk

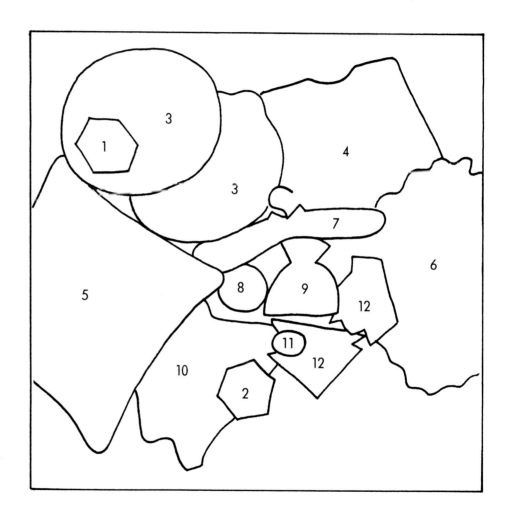

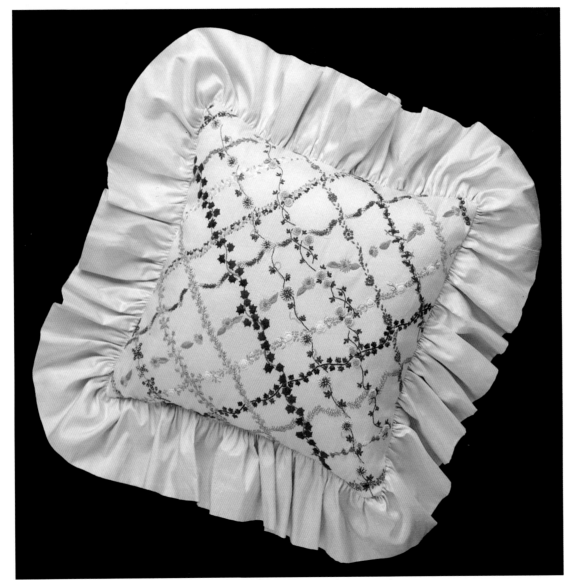

EMBROIDERED CUSHION

108

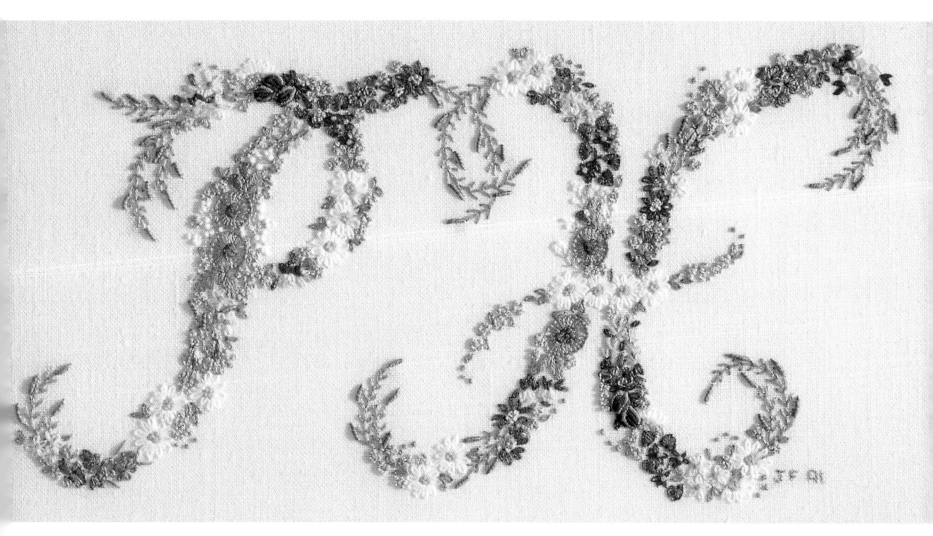

EMBROIDERED INITIALS

GARRYA (TASSEL BUSH) *Garrya elliptica*

THREADS

613 drab brown — light
3013 khaki green — light
778 antique mauve — very light
3051 grey green — dark
936 avocado green — very dark

STRANDS, STITCHES AND NEEDLES

leaves   2 strands 3051, lazy daisy stitch, crewel 8
tassels   2 strands 936, 1 strand each 613 and 3013
                       blended, coral stitch, crewel 8
                       1 strand each 3013 and 778 blended, coral stitch,
                       crewel 8

leaves
lazy daisy stitch

tassels
coral stitch

Lightly mark the outline shape for the Garrya. Work leaves with the two shades of green in lazy daisy stitch all over the area you have outlined, but not too densely because you will add more after the tassels have been worked. The tassels are worked over the leaves with coral stitch in both of the above combinations. Each tassel is formed by working two or three lengths of coral stitch starting at the same point. Each length will have three coral stitches, but the length of each should vary slightly. Add extra leaves to fill spaces and above each tassel.

GRAPE HYACINTH *Muscari armeniacum*

THREADS
333   blue violet – dark
3052   green grey – medium

STRANDS, STITCHES AND NEEDLES
stems   2 strands 3052, couching, crewel 8
flowers   2 strands 333, French knots, crewel 8

Lightly mark stems and couch. Work French knots down either side and over the stem starting at the peak and increasing to the base, forming an elongated conical shape. Do not work these flowers too closely together as they tend to lose their shape and become just a blur of blue.

flowers
French knots

stems
couching

GYPSOPHILA (BABY'S BREATH) *Gypsophila elegans*

THREADS
Blanc neige
3347   yellow green – medium

STRANDS, STITCHES AND NEEDLES
foliage   1 strand 3347, fly stitch, crewel 9
flowers   2 strands blanc neige, French knots, crewel 8

Lightly mark an area for the foliage and work in fly stitch. Flowers are worked in clusters of French knots at the top of the foliage, with more scattered throughout.

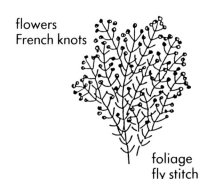

flowers
French knots

foliage
fly stitch

HEARTSEASE *or* JOHNNY JUMP-UP
Viola tricolor (Kardinal Rose garden)

If you look closely at a heartsease plant in the garden you'll find the intensity of colour varies considerably from flower to flower. The newly opened flowers are vibrant and those which have been out for a while have faded to softer hues. Try other thread combinations for even more variety using the threads listed.

leaves – lazy
daisy stitch

THREADS
208	lavender – very dark
210	lavender – medium
211	lavender – light
333	blue violet – very dark
444	lemon – dark
469	avocado green
550	violet – very dark
726	topaz – light
727	topaz – very light

△ ▷ △   start➤ ⌂ ꙮ

spot – French
knot

upper side petals –
lazy daisy stitch

lower petals –
buttonhole stitch

STRANDS, STITCHES AND NEEDLES

lower petal vibrant   2 strands 444, buttonhole stitch crewel 8

            faded   1 strand each 444 and 726 blended, buttonhole stitch, crewel 8

top petals and spot

            vibrant   2 strands 550, lazy daisy stitch and French knot crewel 8

            faded   1 strand each 208 and 333 blended, lazy daisy stitch and French knot, crewel 8

side petals	1 strand each 727 and 211 blended *or* two strands 210, lazy daisy stitch, crewel 8
leaves	2 strands 469, lazy daisy stitch, crewel 8

These flowers are very tiny, so the stitches need to be kept as small as possible. Work one or two flowers at a time in each thread combination. This makes it easier to position the flowers. Some flowers may overlap another. Be sure to keep all threads on the top of your work whilst working.

Draw small triangles for the lower petals. Work each lower petal with three tiny buttonhole stitches. Start stitching at the left-hand side of the lower edge and work each stitch into the same hole (in the centre of the flower).

From slightly above the central point, work the two top petals (pointing upwards) in lazy daisy stitch. Add the spot with a French knot to the bottom edge of the lower petal. Work the side petals at a slightly upward angle. They will overlap the upper petals a little.

Work leaves with lazy daisy stitch beneath and amongst the flowers.

HEARTSEASE (JOHNNY JUMP-UP) *Viola tricolor*

THREADS

444	lemon — dark	
211	lavender — light	
727	topaz — very light	
550	violet — very dark	
469	avocado green	

STRANDS, STITCHES AND NEEDLES

flowers	lower petals	2 strands 444, buttonhole stitch, crewel 8
	top petals	2 strands 550, lazy daisy stitch, crewel 8
	spot	2 strands 550, French knot, crewel 8
	side petals	1 strand each 727 and 211 blended, lazy daisy stitch, crewel 8
leaves		2 strands 469, lazy daisy stitch, crewel 8

These flowers are very tiny, so the stitches need to be kept as small as possible. Begin with the lower petal, using three buttonhole stitches. From the same central point, work the two top petals pointing upwards in lazy daisy stitch. Add the flower spot with a French knot on the bottom edge of the lower petal. Work the side petals at a slightly upward angle. Leaves in lazy daisy stitch are scattered at random amongst the flowers.

leaves
lazy daisy stitch

flower
— upper petals — lazy daisy stitch
— lower petal — buttonhole stitch
— spot — French knot
start

HOLLYHOCK *Alcea rosea* (previously *Althaea rosea*)

THREADS

3335	rose
962	dusty rose – medium
3364	pine green

STRANDS, STITCHES AND NEEDLES

flowers	outer petals	2 strands 962, buttonhole stitch, crewel 8
	centres	3 strands 335, French knots, crewel 7
	buds	2 strands 3364, French knots, 2 twists, crewel 8
		2 strands 335, French knots, 2 twists, crewel 8
opening flower		2 strands, 335, 5 buttonhole stitches, crewel 8
calyx		2 strands 3364, fly stitch, crewel 8
stem		2 strands 3364, stem stitch, crewel 8
leaves		2 strands 3364, satin leaf stitch, crewel 8

Lightly mark stem and then placement of flowers – an inner and outer circle graduating in size from large at the base to smaller at the top. These flowers are not completely circular but slightly irregular in shape. Work outer circle in buttonhole stitch and inner circle in French knots.

Work stem in stem stitch from the base upwards, connecting each flower head. Two rows can be worked for the lower stem. Extend the stem; hollyhocks are very tall plants and can grow to 2.5 metres (8').

Sew the buds with French knots (two twists) alternating the colours of green and pink around the top of the stem.

The uppermost opening flowers are worked with a segment of buttonhole stitch (five stitches) attached to the stem with a calyx in fly stitch. It is easier to turn your work upside down to sew these half-opened flowers.

Leaves are worked in satin leaf stitch at the base of your hollyhock, with smaller ones between the flowers.

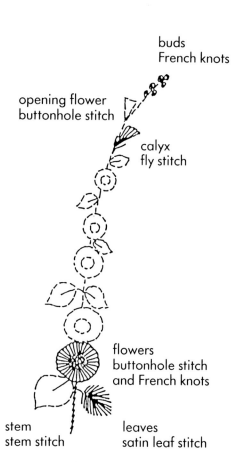

buds
French knots

opening flower
buttonhole stitch

calyx
fly stitch

flowers
buttonhole stitch
and French knots

stem
stem stitch

leaves
satin leaf stitch

HYDRANGEA *Hydrangea macrophylla*

THREADS
340   blue violet — medium
341   blue violet — light
209   lavender — dark
211   lavender — light
3348   yellow green — light
3346   hunter green

STRANDS, STITCHES AND NEEDLES

flowers   centre   4 strands blended in different combinations of 340, 341, 209 and 211, colonial knots, crewel 7
             outside   3 strands blended in different combinations of 340, 341, 209 and 211, colonial knots, crewel 7
new flowers   1 strand each 3348, 211 and 340 blended, colonial knots, crewel 7
leaves   2 strands 3346, satin leaf stitch, crewel 8

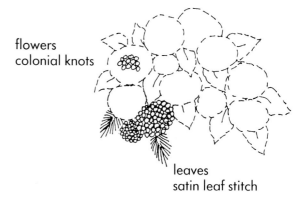

flowers
colonial knots

leaves
satin leaf stitch

Draw circular or elliptical flower shapes with leaves between to form a bush. Vary the intensity and the colour of the flowers by blending the threads.

Work the centre of the flower with four strands in colonial knots. Complete the flower shape with colonial knots in three strands. Stitch colonial knots in formation; ie, rows across or around the flower rather than higgledy-piggledy. The new flowers are smaller and worked entirely with three strands.

Work the leaves between the flowers with satin leaf stitch.

HYDRANGEA *Hydrangea macrophylla* Autumn

THREADS
223   shell pink — light
3348   yellow green — light
3346   hunter green
3347   yellow green — medium

STRANDS, STITCHES AND NEEDLES

flowers	centre	4 strands blended in different combinations of 223 and 3348, colonial knots, crewel 7
	outside	3 strands blended in different combinations of 223 and 3348, colonial knots, crewel 7
leaves		2 strands 3346, satin leaf stitch, crewel 8
		2 strands 3347, satin leaf stitch, crewel 8

Draw circular or elliptical flower shapes with leaves between to form a bush. Vary the colour of the flowers by blending the threads; some of the flowers should feature more pink and others more green. Work the centre of the flower with four strands in colonial knots. Complete the flower shape with colonial knots in three strands. Stitch colonial knots in formation; ie, rows across or around the flower rather than higgledy-piggledy.

Work the leaves between the flowers with satin leaf stitch.

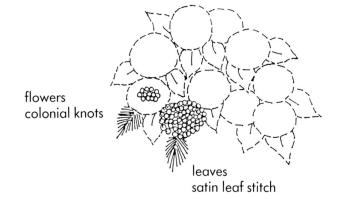

flowers
colonial knots

leaves
satin leaf stitch

ITALIAN LAVENDER *Lavandula stoechas*

THREADS

208	lavender – very dark
522	fern green
550	violet – very dark
3740	antique violet – dark

STRANDS, STITCHES AND NEEDLES

branches and foliage	2 strands 522, fly stitch, crewel 8
stems	1 strand each 522 and 3740 blended, straight stitch, crewel 8
flower heads	1 strand each 550 and 3740 blended, bullion stitch (five wraps), crewel 8
bracts	2 strands 208, straight stitch, crewel 8

stems –
straight stitch

bracts –
straight stitch

flower heads –
bullion stitch

branches and
foliage – fly
stitch

Lightly mark the branches for the foliage. Start at the top of the bush and work each branch with fly stitch down to the 'ground'. Overlap some branches and stitch some smaller branches for a well-shaped bush. The fly stitch branches can only be worked down so you will have to finish off your thread at the 'ground' and start again. You can weave a short distance up the back for the smaller branches.

Work straight stitch stems (5mm, ¼") for the flowers at the top of the bush and amongst the foliage.

Work the flower heads, with bullion stitch attached to each stem.

Add the petal-like bracts above each flower head with two or three small straight stitches.

JAPANESE ANEMONE (WINDFLOWER) *Anemone hupehensis*

THREADS

3689	mauve — light	
472	avocado green — ultra light	
742	tangerine — light	
470	avocado green — light	

STRANDS, STITCHES AND NEEDLES

flowers	centre	4 strands 472, French knot, crewel 7
	petals	2 strands 3689, lazy daisy stitch, crewel 8
	stamens	1 strand 742, French knots, crewel 9
stems		1 strand 470, couching, crewel 9
leaves		2 strands 470, lazy daisy and double lazy daisy stitch, crewel 8

The flowers are worked first. The centre is a French knot with four strands of 472. Stitch a few extra flower centres to depict the forming seed heads. Leave a little space around the centre for the stamens to be added after the petals. Work several lazy daisy stitch petals and add the stamens with French knots around the centre. Some half flowers add interest.

Work the stems with couching, joining the seed heads and flowers. The leaves splay from the stems and are formed by working two or three lazy daisy and double lazy daisy stitches together, pointing downwards.

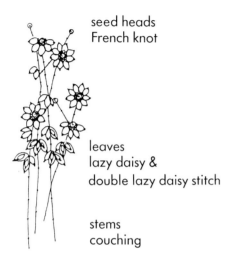

seed heads
French knot

leaves
lazy daisy &
double lazy daisy stitch

stems
couching

flower
lazy daisy stitch
centre — French knots

JONQUIL (CREAM) 'Grande Monarque' *Narcissus tazetta*

THREADS
445   lemon — light
746   off white
3363   pine green — medium

STRANDS, STITCHES AND NEEDLES
stems   2 strands 3363, stem stitch, crewel 8
leaves   2 strands 3363, stem stitch, crewel 8
flowers   centre   3 strands 445, French knot, crewel 7
               petals   2 strands 746, French knot stalks, crewel 8

Mark the stems and leaves and work in stem stitch. Stitch four or five French knot centres above each stem, leaving room for the petals. Add six French knot petals around each centre to form a cluster of flowers. The petals are worked with a French knot stalk with a short tail; start a little distance from the centre and finish with the knot touching the centre.

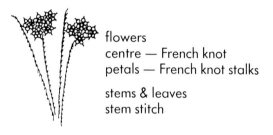

flowers
centre — French knot
petals — French knot stalks

stems & leaves
stem stitch

JONQUIL (YELLOW) 'Grand Soleil d'Or' *Narcissus tazetta*

THREADS
307   lemon
741   tangerine — medium
3363   pine green — medium

STRANDS, STITCHES AND NEEDLES

stems		2 strands 3363, stem stitch, crewel 8
leaves		2 strands 3363, stem stitch, crewel 8
flowers	centre	3 strands 741, French knots, crewel 7
	petals	2 strands 307, French knots, crewel 8

Mark the stems and leaves and work in stem stitch. Stitch four or five French knot centres above each stem, leaving room for the petals. Add the six French knot petals around each centre to form a cluster of flowers.

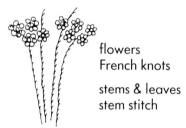

flowers
French knots

stems & leaves
stem stitch

'KARDINAL' ROSA X *Hybrid Tea Rose*

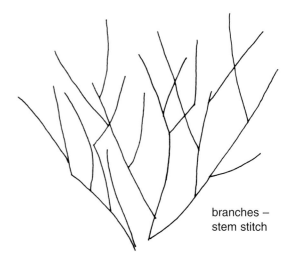

branches –
stem stitch

THREADS

611	drab brown – dark
814	garnet – dark
815	garnet – medium
936	avocado green – very dark
3346	hunter green

STRANDS, STITCHES AND NEEDLES

branches	2 strands 611, stem stitch, crewel 8
full-blown rose	2 strands 815, buttonhole stitch, crewel 8
	1 strand each 814 and 815 blended, buttonhole stitch, crewel 8
buds	1 strand each 814 and 815, lazy daisy stitch, crewel 8
stems	2 strands 3346, couching, crewel 8
thorns:	1 strand 3346, backstitch, crewel 9
leaf stalks	2 strands 936, backstitch, crewel 8
leaves:	2 strands 936, lazy daisy stitch, crewel 8
sepals	2 strands 936, fly and straight stitch, crewel 8

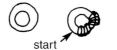

start

rose –
buttonhole stitch

buds – lazy
daisy stitch

Mark the branches for the rose. Work the major branches with two rows of stem stitch and smaller branches with one.

Before you begin the roses, thread up all the needles you require. Work several roses and buds amongst the branches.

Mark a circle for the rose with a small circle within. Work each petal from the inside circle with three or four buttonhole stitches forming a scallop shape. The first stitch will look like a lazy daisy stitch. Take the

sepals – fly stitch or
straight stitch

stems –
couching

leaf stalks –
back stitch

leaves – lazy
daisy stitch

thread to the back of your work to complete the petal.

Work five petals (more for a bigger rose) around the circle with 815, and then work three or four inner petals to overlap the first with 814/815. If you have a little space left in the centre and can't fit another petal, fill with a French knot.

Add several rose buds amongst the branches and roses.Work each bud with four lazy daisy stitches to form a nicely shaped bud. Work two lazy daisy stitches side by side; from the middle of these add another lazy daisy to form the tip of the bud. Work the fourth lazy daisy from below the bud into the centre of the bud.

Add stems to all roses and buds attaching them back to the branches with couching.

Add thorns to the stems and branches with tiny backstitches, angled down from the stem.

Work curving stalks for the leaves with three or four small backstitches.

Add lazy daisy stitch leaves in pairs along the stalks and one for the tip (five to seven leaves).

Work a tiny fly stitch or straight stitches around each bud and a straight stitch into the bud depicting the sepals.

Add stalks and leaves to the branches amongst the roses and buds stitching over existing embroidery.

KUMQUAT *Fortunella margarita*

THREADS

741   tangerine — medium
3346   hunter green
611   drab brown — dark
612   drab brown — medium
731   olive green — dark

STRANDS, STITCHES AND NEEDLES

tree   2 strands 611, stem stitch, crewel 8
                  1 strand each 611 and 612 blended, crewel 8
                  2 strands 612, stem stitch, crewel 8
twigs   1 strand 731, fly stitch and couching, crewel 9
leaves   2 strands 3346, lazy daisy stitch, crewel 8
fruit   4 strands 741, French knots (2 twists), crewel 7

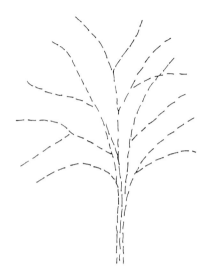

Draw in the trunk and major branches of the tree and work in stem stitch in 611. Sew a second row for the trunk in stem stitch with blended 611 and 612. Add a third row for the trunk and work some branches in 612.

The twigs are added to the branches with a fly stitch with a long tail, which is couched into position. The leaves in lazy daisy stitch are worked all over the branches and twigs and the fruit is added with French knots (two twists).

twigs
fly stitch & couching

branches
stem stitch

fruit
French knot

leaves
lazy daisy stitch

LAMB'S EAR *Stachys byzantina*

THREADS
209   lavender — dark
648   beaver grey — light

STRANDS, STITCHES AND NEEDLES

stems	2 strands 648, whipped stem stitch, crewel 8
minor stems	2 strands 648, stem stitch, crewel 8
leaves	2 strands 648, bullion stitch (9 and 11 wraps), straw 8
small leaves	2 strands 648, bullion stitch (4 wraps), straw 8
buds	2 strands 648, French knots, crewel 8
flowers	2 strands 648 and 1 strand 209 blended, French knots, crewel 8

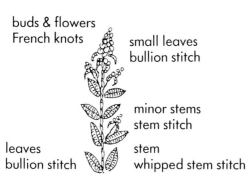

buds & flowers
French knots

small leaves
bullion stitch

minor stems
stem stitch

leaves
bullion stitch

stem
whipped stem stitch

Study the illustration carefully and thread up with the different thread combinations before you begin. Pencil in the stems and work with whipped stem stitch. Add minor stems with stem stitch. At the tip of the plant stitch some buds with French knots and then some flowers. Add small leaves amongst and just below the flowers.

Leaves are worked down the stem in pairs and on the ground. Each leaf is formed with two bullion stitches side by side.

LILY-OF-THE-VALLEY *Convallaria majalis*

THREADS
Blanc neige
3347   yellow green – medium

STRANDS, STITCHES AND NEEDLES
flowers   2 strands blanc neige, French knots, crewel 8
stems   1 strand 3347, stem stitch, crewel 9
leaves   2 strands 3347, satin stitch, crewel 8, outlined in 1 strand
             stem stitch, crewel 9

Lightly mark arched stem and two leaves. Leaves are worked in a very slanting satin stitch and are outlined with one strand of stem stitch. Work stems in stem stitch and add French knot flowers over the stem.

stems
stem stitch

flowers
French knots

leaves
satin stitch
outline – stem stitch

LOVE-IN-A-MIST *Nigella damascena*

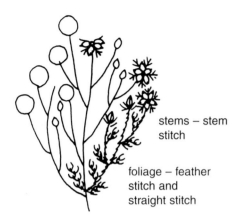

stems – stem
stitch

foliage – feather
stitch and
straight stitch

sepals –
straight stitch

flowers – lazy
daisy stitch

centre –
French knot

buds – straight
stitch and lazy
daisy stitch

THREADS

793	cornflower blue – medium
3347	yellow green – medium
3363	pine green – medium
3740	antique violet – dark

STRANDS, STITCHES AND NEEDLES

stems	young stems	1 strand 3347, stem stitch, crewel 9
	mature stems	1 strand each 3347 and 3363 blended, stem stitch, crewel 8
flowers	petals	2 strands 793, lazy daisy stitch, crewel 8
	centre	1 strand each 3740 and 3363 blended, French knot, crewel 8
buds		1 strand each 3347 and 3363 blended, lazy daisy and straight stitch, crewel 8
sepals and foliage		1 strand 3347, feather stitch and straight stitch, crewel 9
pods		1 strand each 3740 and 3363 blended, bullion stitch, crewel 8
spikes		1 strand 3347, crewel 9

Draw stems and work them with stem stitch in the thread combinations above.

Work the five petalled flowers with small lazy daisy stitches, leaving a space for the centre. Add some side-view flowers with just four petals.

Add French knot (two twists) to the centre of flowers.

Add a few buds to some of the minor branches. Work a small straight stitch with a lazy daisy stitch around it.

Add straight stitch sepals for flowers to the gaps between petals, and for buds from the stem just below.

Add the tufts of foliage quite freely to the stems with feather stitch and the odd straight stitch. To achieve the effect of flowers peeping through a ferny mist, work an occasional stitch over a flower.

Add some pods to the plant if you wish, with 2 bullion stitches (three or four wraps) side by side, with three or four spikes above.

Feather stitch

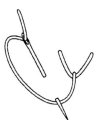
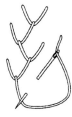

1.   2.   3.

MAGNOLIA *Magnolia x soulangeana*

THREADS
Blanc neige

316	antique mauve – medium
839	beige brown – dark
840	beige brown – medium
3013	khaki green – light

STRANDS, STITCHES AND NEEDLES

tree	2 strands 839, stem stitch, crewel 8
	2 strands 840, stem stitch, crewel 8
flowers	2 strands blanc neige and 1 strand 316 blended, double lazy daisy stitch, crewel 7
calyxes	2 strands 3013, fly stitch, crewel 8
leaf buds	2 strands 3013, bullion stitch, straw 8

Draw in the trunk and branches of the tree and work in stem stitch in 839. Sew a second row in 840 stem stitch for the trunk and major branches. A third row in 840 may be added for the trunk if desired.

Flowers are worked in large, loose, double lazy daisy stitch with the stitches overlapping. Some should have three petals, and some four, for variation. A straight stitch can be added if there is a gap in the centre of the double lazy daisy stitch.

Attach flowers to branches with a calyx in fly stitch. Scatter leaf buds over the tree, worked in bullion stitch (nine wraps), anchoring the thread further out to form an elongated point.

flowers
double lazy daisy
and straight stitch

leaf buds
bullion stitch

calyx
fly stitch

branches
stem stitch

NANDINA (DWARF) 'Nana' *Nandina domestica*

THREADS
347   salmon — very dark
3721   shell pink — dark
3347   yellow green — medium

STRANDS, STITCHES AND NEEDLES
foliage   2 strands 3347, lazy daisy stitch, crewel 8
                       2 strands 347, lazy daisy stitch, crewel 8
                       2 strands 3721, lazy daisy stitch, crewel 8
                       1 strand each 347 and 3721 blended, lazy daisy
                       stitch, crewel 8

Pencil in a dome shape for the outline of the bush. Cover the area with lazy daisy stitches in each of the above combinations. The stitches should point in different directions.

leaves
lazy daisy stitch

NERINE *Nerine bowdenii*

THREADS
603   cranberry
604   cranberry — light
3347 yellow green — medium

STRANDS, STITCHES AND NEEDLES

stems	2 strands 3347, whipped stem stitch, crewel 8
flower stalks	1 strand 3347, straight stitch, crewel 9
flowers	1 strand each 603 and 604 blended, fly stitch, crewel 8

Lightly mark the stems and work in whipped stem stitch. Place several flower stalks coming from the top of the stem in straight stitch. The flowers are worked in fly stitch with a small 'V' on the outside of the flower. The long tail goes into the same hole in the centre over the flower stalks. Work in a clockwise direction and stagger the length of the stitches.

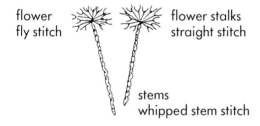

flower
fly stitch

flower stalks
straight stitch

stems
whipped stem stitch

ORNAMENTAL GRAPE *Vilis alicante* Autumn

THREADS
347   salmon — very dark
221   shell pink — very dark
640   beige grey — very dark

STRANDS, STITCHES AND NEEDLES
vine   2 strands 640, stem stitch, crewel 8
leaves   2 strands 347, straight stitch, crewel 8
                        2 strands 221, straight stitch, crewel 8
                        1 strand each 347 and 221 blended, straight
                        stitch, crewel 8

Pencil in the vine entwined around the arch. Work in stem stitch. Add
the leaves around the vine pointing in different directions. Scatter two
or three on the ground. Vary the size of the leaves and stitch them
in the three different thread combinations listed above. Check the
illustration before working the leaves. Start at the top left-hand side
of the leaf and, with straight stitches, work from the outside, with all
the stitches going into the same hole in the centre. Work three short
stitches, then one long stitch, all around the leaf. Finish with three short
stitches.

vine
stem stitch

leaves
straight stitch

CHARLOTTE'S STORY

I designed this embroidered flower especially for my daughter Charlotte and I would like to share this delightful and romantic story with you. When she was fifteen, Charlotte was walking home from school with her first boyfriend Peter. He picked a passionflower and gave it to her. Neither of them knew what the flower was at the time but they were both fascinated with its exotic beauty.

Peter moved away to another city the following year. Charlotte received a letter much later from him and when she opened the envelope, out fell a pressed passionflower. Charlotte invited Peter to be her partner for her end of school formal party. He combed the gardens of friends to find some passionflowers, then took them to a florist and had them made into a corsage for her and a buttonhole for himself. How thrilled she was when he presented this to her. They seldom see each other these days, but remain close friends and the passionflower symbolises this friendship.

As a surprise for Charlotte I embroidered her initial with passionflowers for her 21st birthday.

flower
petals — lazy daisy bullion stitch

corona — straight stitch
stamens — French knots

PASSIONFLOWER *Passiflora caerulea*

THREADS

ecru
369   pistachio green — very light
333   blue violet — very dark
726   topaz — light
3364 pine green
327   violet — very dark
3362 pine green — dark

centre — bullion stitch

STRANDS, STITCHES AND NEEDLES

flowers	petals	1 strand each ecru and 369 blended, lazy daisy bullion stitch (4 wraps), straw 8
	corona	1 strand 333, straight stitch, crewel 9
	stamens	1 strand each 726 and 3364 blended, French knots, crewel 8
	centre	1 strand 327, bullion stitch, straw 9
leaves		2 strands 3362, double lazy daisy stitch, crewel 8
buds		2 strands 3364, lazy daisy stitch, crewel 8
tendrils		1 strand 3364, stem stitch or back stitch, crewel 9
stems		2 strands 3364, stem stitch, crewel 8

Lightly mark flowers with a small circle surrounded by a larger circle. Ten petals are worked in lazy daisy bullion stitch (4 wraps) in the outer circle. To help space the petals, work the hour and half-hour stitches first. Then space the four stitches on each side as evenly as possible.

The corona is added with violet blue straight stitches between and into each petal. Four French knots form the stamens which fill the centre with the blended yellow and green. The final touch to the centre of the flower is worked in purple with two bullion stitches to form a 'Y'. First, work a bullion with eight wraps across the centre of the flower. Then, work a second bullion with only four wraps from the middle of the first bullion to the outside of the circle, forming a 'Y'.

The buds are worked with three slightly overlapping lazy daisy stitches. Stems can be worked in stem stitch if required. The climbing tendrils are worked with stem stitch or back stitch. Finally, the palmate leaves are worked with five double lazy daisy stitches.

bud
lazy daisy stitch

tendrils
stem or back stitch

leaves
double lazy daisy stitch

PENCIL PINE *Cupressus sempervirens*

THREADS

3362   pine green — dark
3363   pine green — medium
3346   hunter green
610   drab brown — very dark
611   drab brown — dark

STRANDS, STITCHES AND NEEDLES

foliage	1 strand each 3362 and 3363 blended, straight stitch, crewel 8
	1 strand each 3362 and 3346 blended, straight stitch, crewel 8
	1 strand each 3363 and 3346 blended, straight stitch crewel 8
nuts	2 strands each 610 and 611 blended, French knot (2 twists), crewel 7

Note: Use a small hoop for good tension when working straight stitch.

Pencil in the outline of the tree. Thread up your needles in the different thread combinations. Cover the area with straight stitches of varying length in each of the above combinations. Some of the stitches should be on a slight angle. Add the nuts to complete your pencil pine.

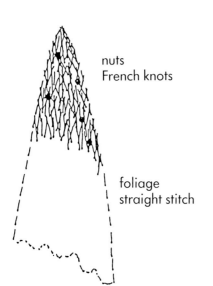

nuts
French knots

foliage
straight stitch

PENSTEMON *Penstemon davisonii*

THREADS

315   antique mauve — very dark
3350   dusty rose — ultra dark
988   forest green — medium

STRANDS, STITCHES AND NEEDLES

stems   2 strands 315, couching, crewel 8
flowers   2 strands 3350, lazy daisy stitch and buttonhole
                                 stitch, crewel 8
leaves   2 strands 988, bullion stitch (7 wraps), straw 8

Pencil in and work the arching stems with couching. Add the flowers with a couple of lazy daisy stitches at the tip of the stem and several bells of two buttonhole stitches down the stem. The leaves are worked at random up the stems in pairs using bullion stitches.

flowers
lazy daisy & buttonhole stitch

stems
couching

leaves
bullion stitch

PERIWINKLE *Vinca major*

THREADS
209   lavender – dark
3346   hunter green

STRANDS, STITCHES AND NEEDLES
stems   2 strands 3346, couching, crewel 8
leaves   2 strands 3346, lazy daisy stitch, crewel 8
flowers   2 strands 209, lazy daisy stitch, crewel 8
buds   1 strand 209, bullion stitch, straw 9

Lightly mark stems and stitch in couching. Work lazy daisy stitch leaves in pairs along stems. Work flowers of fine petals in small lazy daisy stitch at the top of the stem and scatter a few through the foliage. Place the occasional bud using bullion stitch (nine wraps). Extend the needle out slightly when anchoring the bullion, to give an elongated and curved effect.

buds
bullion stitch

flowers
lazy daisy stitch

stems
couching

leaves
lazy daisy stitch

PETUNIA *Petunia velutina*

THREADS
3746   blue violet — dark
3347   yellow green — medium
3052   green grey — medium

STRANDS, STITCHES AND NEEDLES
flowers   2 strands 3746, buttonhole stitch, crewel 8
leaves   1 strand each 3347 and 3052 blended, lazy daisy
                     stitch, crewel 8

Work the flowers with small circles of buttonhole stitch. Add lazy daisy
stitch leaves underneath and between the flowers.

flowers
buttonhole stitch

leaves
lazy daisy stitch

PINKS *Dianthus plumarius*

THREADS

3685	mauve – dark
3687	mauve
503	blue green – medium
522	fern green

STRANDS, STITCHES AND NEEDLES

flowers	petals	2 strands 3687, straight stitch, crewel 8
	flecks	2 strands 3685, back stitch, crewel 8
stems		1 strand each 503 and 522 blended, stem stitch, crewel 8
leaves and stalks		1 strand each 503 and 522 blended, straight stitch, crewel 8
buds		2 strands 3687, lazy daisy stitch, crewel 8

petals – straight stitch
flecks – backstitch

buds – lazy daisy stitch

stems – stem stitch

leaves and stalks for buds – straight stitch

Draw small circles with a dot in the centre for the flowers. Work the flowers with straight stitch from the outside edge down into the centre. All stitches are worked into the same hole in the centre. Don't work too many stitches for each flower and vary the length of the stitches to achieve a ragged edge like a carnation.

Add flecks of deep pink around centre of flower with tiny backstitch. Work short stems for the flowers with stem stitch.

Add straight stitch leaves up and down the stems and from the ground, forming a clump. Some of these straight stitches will form the stalks for buds.

Add some buds to the stalks with lazy daisy stitch.

POLYANTHUS *Primula X polyantha*

Note: Two colours are given for this flower.

THREADS
340   blue violet — medium
307   lemon
or
743   yellow — medium
741   tangerine — medium

469   avacado green — light
471   avacado green — very light

STRANDS, STITCHES AND NEEDLES
flowers   2 strands 340 or 743, buttonhole stitch, crewel 8
            centres   2 strands 307 or 741, French knot, crewel 8
stems   2 strands 471, couching, crewel 8
leaves   2 strands 469, lazy daisy stitch, crewel 8

Work the flowers in small circles of buttonhole stitch with French knot centres. Add the stems with couching and the leaves below in lazy daisy stitch.

flowers
buttonhole stitch
centre — French knot
stems
couching
leaves
lazy daisy stitch

PRIMULA *Primula malacoides*

THREADS
blanc neige
3347   yellow green — medium

STRANDS, STITCHES AND NEEDLES
leaves   1 strand 3347, buttonhole stitch, crewel 9
stems   1 strand 3347, couching, crewel 9
flowers   2 strands blanc neige, French knots, crewel 8

Mark the small circular leaves and work them in buttonhole stitch. Add the stems above the leaves with couching. Work the flowers with clusters of French knots at the top of the stem and halfway down the stem.

stems
couching
flowers
French knots
leaves
buttonhole stitch

ROSE 'Rosamunde' *Rosa X*

rose
centre — French knots
petals — bullion stitch

THREADS

972	canary	— deep
3708	melon	— light
776	pink	— medium
819	baby pink	— light
3051	green grey	— dark

STRANDS, STITCHES AND NEEDLES

rose	centre	2 strands 972, French knots, crewel 8
rose		2 strands 3708, bullion stitch (7 wraps), straw 8
		2 strands 776, bullion stitch (9 wraps), straw 8
		2 strands 819, bullion stitch (11 wraps), straw 8
buds		2 strands 3708, bullion stitch (7 wraps), straw 8
calyx		2 strands 3051, fly stitch, crewel 8
stems		2 strands 3051, coral stitch, crewel 8
leaves		2 strands 3051, double lazy daisy stitch, crewel 8

buds — bullion stitch
calyx — fly stitch
sepals — straight stitch

leaves
double lazy daisy stitch
leaf stems — coral stitch

Embroider the rose centre with five French knots. Then, with 3708, work three bullion stitches (7 wraps) around the centre. Next, with 776, work five bullion stitches (9 wraps) overlapping around the rose. Finally, with 819, work approximately seven bullion stitches (11 wraps) for the outer petals, again overlapping until a well-balanced rose is formed.

Add the buds with two bullion stitches placed side by side. Work a fly stitch calyx around the buds and two sepals with straight stitches on the tip of the buds.

Stems for the leaves are worked with coral stitch and the leaves are added in pairs of double lazy daisy stitch with one for the tip (five to seven leaves).

ROSE 'Peter Frankenfeld' *Rosa* X

THREADS

602	cranberry — medium
603	cranberry
604	cranberry — light
3051	green grey — dark
611	drab brown — dark

STRANDS, STITCHES AND NEEDLES

branches	2 strands 611, stem stitch, crewel 8
rose	2 strands 602, bullion stitch (7 wraps), straw 8
	2 strands 603, bullion stitch (9 wraps), straw 8
	2 strands 604, bullion stitch (11 wraps), straw 8
buds	2 strands 602, bullion stitch (7 wraps), straw 8
calyx	2 strands 3051, fly stitch, crewel 8
stems	2 strands 3051, coral stitch, crewel 8
leaves	2 strands 3051, lazy daisy stitch, crewel 8

Mark the trunk and branches of the rose bush and work the trunk with two rows of stem stitch and one row for the branches. Several full-blown roses are then worked among the branches. Start in the centre with the deepest pink 602 and work three bullion stitches (7 wraps) side by side. Then, with 603, work five bullion stitches (9 wraps) overlapping around the centre. Finally, with 604, work approximately five bullions (11 wraps) for the outer petals. Try to vary the look of each rose by arranging the bullion stitches in a different way.

Add several buds with two bullion stitches placed side by side. Join the buds to the branches with a fly stitch calyx and work two sepals with straight stitches on the tip of the buds.

Stems for the leaves are worked with coral stitch and the leaves are added in pairs of lazy daisy stitch, with one for the tip (five to seven leaves).

rose
bullion stitch

leaves
lazy daisy stitch
leaf stems — coral stitch

buds — bullion stitch
calyx — fly stitch
sepals — straight stitch

branches
stem stitch

ROSE CAMPION *Lychnis coronia*

THREADS
718   plum
504   blue green — light

STRANDS, STITCHES AND NEEDLES

flowers	1 strand 718, buttonhole stitch, crewel 9
buds	1 strand 718, bullion stitch (9 wraps), straw 9
	1 strand 504, bullion stitch (9 wraps), straw 9
calyx	2 strands 504, fly stitch, crewel 8
stems	2 strands 504, coral stitch, crewel 8
leaves	2 strands 504, lazy daisy stitch, crewel 8

Work small buttonhole circles for the flowers and some half circles to depict a side-on view. The stems are worked next with coral stitch. Attach them to the flowers and make some extra branches for the buds. Add a few buds in plum and a few in blue green with bullion stitch (nine wraps). Attach the buds to the stems with a fly stitch. Work the leaves in pairs with lazy daisy stitches coming from the stems.

buds
bullion stitch
calyx — fly stitch

flowers
buttonhole stitch

stems
coral stitch

leaves
lazy daisy stitch

ROSEHIPS *Rosa sp.*

THREADS
349   coral — dark
611   drab brown — dark

STRANDS, STITCHES AND NEEDLES

branches	2 strands 611, stem stitch, crewel 8
twigs and thorns	1 strand 611, straight stitch, crewel 9
hips	3 strands 349, French knots, crewel 7

Pencil in the branches and embroider in stem stitch. Add twigs and thorns with straight stitch and the hips with French knots.

hips
French knots

branches
stem stitch

twigs & thorns
straight stitch

ROSE (STANDARD) Rosa

THREADS

221	shell pink – dark
223	shell pink – medium
3051	green grey – dark
937	avocado green – medium

STRANDS, STITCHES AND NEEDLES

trunk		2 strands 3051, stem stitch, crewel 8
flowers	centres	2 strands 221, bullion stitch, straw 8
	outside petals	2 strands 223, bullion stitch, straw 8
leaves		2 strands 3051, lazy daisy stitch, crewel 8
		2 strands 937, lazy daisy stitch, crewel 8

Draw in the trunk approximately 3-4cm (1¼" – 1½") long and mark a circle at the top (a cotton reel is a good size). Work the trunk in two rows of stem stitch.

Mark the placement of roses scattered over the circle – 13 roses are sufficient. Work the centre of roses in two bullion stitches (nine wraps) starting and finishing at the same point at either end. Work bullion stitch outer petals (1 wraps) curving around the centre on either side.

Work lazy daisy leaves in the two shades of green in a sunburst radiating from the centre of the circle to the outside edge. Vary the length and direction of the leaves.

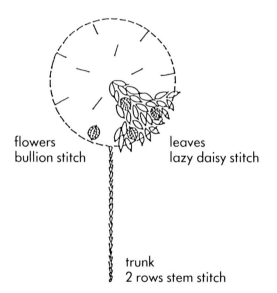

flowers
bullion stitch

leaves
lazy daisy stitch

trunk
2 rows stem stitch

ROSE OF MEXICO or PINK EVENING PRIMROSE
Oenothera speciosa

THREADS

445	lemon – light
471	avocado green – very light
3346	hunter green
3689	mauve – light

STRANDS, STITCHES AND NEEDLES

flowers	petals	1 strand 3689, buttonhole stitch, crewel 9
	centre	2 strands 445, French knot, crewel 8
stems		1 strand 471, stem stitch, crewel 9
buds		1 strand 471, bullion stitch (nine wraps), straw 9
leaves		1 strand 3346, lazy daisy stitch, crewel 9

Draw four petalled flower shapes with a dot in the centre. Stitch each petal from the centre, leaving a tiny space in the centre. Work four or five small buttonhole stitches and then take the needle and thread to the back of your work. The first stitch will look like a lazy daisy stitch. Come up again in the centre to start the next petal and work the other three petals in the same manner. Stitch opposite petals first to make positioning easier.

Add a French knot centre.

Work stems with stem stitch.

Add some buds with bullion stitch amongst the flowers. Work each bud with nine wraps and take the needle out a little further when anchoring the bullion stitch to form a point.

Work the leaves with lazy daisy stitches attached to the stems below the flowers. Leaves should be longish and worked with firm tension to make them thin.

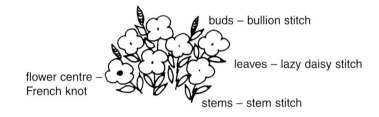

buds – bullion stitch

leaves – lazy daisy stitch

flower centre –
French knot

stems – stem stitch

start

petals – buttonhole stitch

SHASTA DAISY *Chrysanthemum superbum*

THREADS
blanc neige
444   lemon — dark
3347   yellow green — medium

STRANDS, STITCHES AND NEEDLES

flowers	centres	2 strands 444, French knots, crewel 8
	petals	2 strands blanc neige, lazy daisy stitch, crewel 8
stems		2 strands 3347, crewel 8, couching with 1 strand, crewel 9
stem leaves		2 strands 3347, straight stitch, crewel 8
leaves		2 strands 3347, lazy daisy stitch, crewel 8

flowers
centre — French knots
petals — lazy daisy stitch

stem leaves
straight stitch

stems
couching

leaves
lazy daisy stitch

Lightly mark flowers with a small circle surrounded by a larger circle. Work the centre with five French knots. Divide outer circle into quarters like a clock face. Work one lazy daisy stitch petal for each quarter hour, and then fill in between these with more petals. This will prevent a pinwheel effect. The more petals you have, the better it will look. Mark in stems and work in couching. The stem leaves are added with small straight stitches angled downwards and alternating at intervals on each side down the stem. Work leaves with lazy daisy stitches at random around the base. A half flower adds interest.

SILVER BIRCH *Betula pendula*

THREADS
blanc neige
762   pearl grey — very light
611   drab brown — dark

STRANDS, STITCHES AND NEEDLES

trunk and major branches	1 strand each blanc neige and 762 blended, satin stitch, crewel 8
outline	1 strand 611, couching, crewel 9
minor branches	1 strand 611, couching, crewel 9
striations	1 strand 611, straight stitch, crewel 9

Note: For correct tension when couching; use a hoop.

Draw the tree. Work the trunk in a horizontal satin stitch. Work the major branches with a slanting satin stitch. Outline the tree with couching and add the minor branches. Accent the striations with straight stitches of varying widths down the trunk.

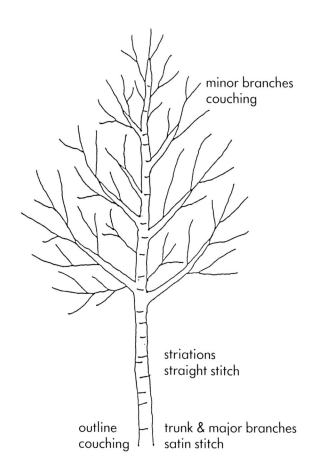

minor branches
couching

striations
straight stitch

outline
couching

trunk & major branches
satin stitch

SOLOMON'S SEAL *Polygonatum multiflorum*

THREADS
Blanc neige
3348   yellow green – light
3347   yellow green – medium

STRANDS, STITCHES AND NEEDLES
stems	2 strands 3347, stem stitch, crewel 8
leaves	2 strands 3347, lazy daisy stitch, crewel 8
flower stalks	1 strand 3347, straight stitch, crewel 9
flowers	1 strand blanc neige, lazy daisy stitch, crewel 9
flower tip	1 strand 3348, French knots, crewel 9

Mark arched stem and work in stem stitch. Work lazy daisy leaves along the top edge of the stem; there should be approximately 16 leaves. Place very small flower stalks pointing downwards from each of the leaves underneath the arching stem. Work two or three flowers form each flower stalk in lazy daisy stitch pointing downwards. The green flower top is worked with a French knot: bring the needle up inside the flower end of each lazy daisy flower, finishing below the flower.

leaves
lazy daisy stitch

flowers
lazy daisy stitch
tips – French knots
stalks – straight stitch

stem
stem stitch

SNOWFLAKE *Leucojum vernum*

THREADS
blanc neige
3347   yellow green — medium

STRANDS, STITCHES AND NEEDLES

stems and leaves	2 strands 3347, stem stitch, crewel 8
flowers	2 strands blanc neige, lazy daisy stitch, crewel 8
flower spots	1 strand 3347, French knots, crewel 9

Draw in stems and leaves and work in stem stitch. Leaving a little stem free at the top, work very small flowers in 'bunches' of two or three lazy daisy stitches down one side of the stem or over the stem. Place a French knot for the flower spot in each of the lazy daisy petals.

flowers
lazy daisy stitch
spots — French knots

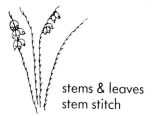

stems & leaves
stem stitch

SUNFLOWER *Helianthus annuus*

flowers
lazy daisy bullion stitch
centre — French knots

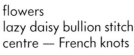

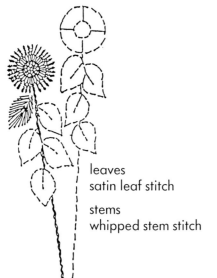

leaves
satin leaf stitch

stems
whipped stem stitch

THREADS

973	canary	— bright
783	topaz	— medium
433	brown	— medium
3347	yellow green	— medium

STRANDS, STITCHES AND NEEDLES

flowers   2 strands 973, lazy daisy bullion stitch (4 wraps), straw 8

     centres   3 strands 783, French knots, crewel 7
                  3 strands 433, French knots, crewel 7

stems   3 strands and 2 strands 3347, whipped stem stitch, crewel 7 and 8

leaves   2 strands 3347, satin leaf stitch, crewel 8

Sunflowers are very tall plants and their faces are always turned towards the sun. Mark flowers in required position with a small circle surrounded by a larger circle. Divide the outer circle into quarters like a clock face. Work one lazy daisy bullion stitch (four wraps) for each quarter hour and then fill in between these with more petals. The more petals you have, the better it will look. Work the centre with French knots in either colour.

Mark the stems and work in whipped stem stitch. The sunflower in the foreground will be stitched with three strands and the others with two strands. Add the leaves with satin leaf stitch, alternating them down each side of the stem. Stitch the occasional leaf over the stem.

VIOLET (SWEET) *Viola odorata*

THREADS
327   violet — very dark
3346   hunter green
743   yellow — medium

STRANDS, STITCHES AND NEEDLES
leaves	1 strand 3346, buttonhole stitch, crewel 9
flowers	1 strand 327, lazy daisy stitch, crewel 9
bud	1 strand 327, lazy daisy stitch, crewel 9
centres	2 strands 743, French knots, crewel 8
calyx	1 strand 3346, fly stitch, crewel 9
stems	1 strand 3346, stem stitch, crewel 9

First work a cluster of heart-shaped leaves in buttonhole stitch. Add the flowers next: they consist of three lazy daisy stitch petals pointing downwards, and two lazy daisy stitch petals pointing upwards. Place a French knot in the centre. Buds have only two lazy daisy stitches pointing downwards, with a calyx of fly stitch. Work stems in stem stitch, arching them at the top where the flower is attached.

flowers
lazy daisy stitch
centre — French knot

stems
stem stitch

buds
lazy daisy stitch

leaves
buttonhole stitch

WALLFLOWER *Cheiranthus mutabilis*

THREADS

3740	antique violet — dark
553	violet
223	shell pink — light
3363	pine green — medium

STRANDS, STITCHES AND NEEDLES

centre buds	1 strand each 3740 and 3363 blended, French knots, crewel 8
flowers	1 strand each 3740 and 553 blended, French knots, crewel 8
	1 strand each 553 and 223 blended, French knots, crewel 8
	1 strand each 3740 and 223 blended, French knots, crewel 8
stems	2 strands 3363, stem stitch, crewel 8
leaves	2 strands 3363, bullion (9 wraps), straw 8

Work the centre buds first with three French knots. Thread up your needles with the three different thread combinations for the flowers and work French knots around the centre buds, forming clusters of flowers.

Work the stems in stem stitch and add the leaves in bullion stitch alternately up the stems.

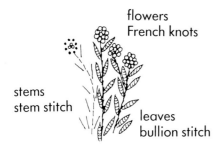

flowers
French knots

stems
stem stitch

leaves
bullion stitch

WATTLE (COOTAMUNDRA) *Acacia baileyana*

THREADS
307   lemon
3787   brown grey — dark
524   fern green — very light

STRANDS, STITCHES AND NEEDLES
tree   2 strands 3787, stem stitch, crewel 8
foliage   2 strands 524, fly stitch, crewel 8
blossom   2 strands 307, French knots, crewel 8

Draw in the trunk and branches of the tree and work in stem stitch. Add a second row of stem stitch for the trunk. The small branches and foliage are created simultaneously with fly stitch. Mark many small branches over the tree and work in fly stitch from the tips back to the main branches. Cover the whole tree heavily with French knots for the blossom; form them into small bunches with three or four French knots worked between the fly stitches.

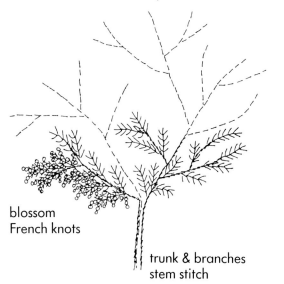

small branches & foliage
fly stitch

blossom
French knots

trunk & branches
stem stitch

WINTER IRIS *Iris stylosa*

THREADS
340   blue violet — medium
209   lavender — dark
3347   yellow green — medium

STRANDS, STITCHES AND NEEDLES

leaves and stems	1 strand 3347, couching, crewel 9
	2 strands 3347, couching, crewel 8
flowers	1 strand each 340 and 209 blended, lazy daisy stitch, crewel 8

Using a hoop, work leaves and stems in couching. First, stitch long leaves with one strand of green. Then add more leaves with two strands until a clump is formed. Flowers are stitched over the leaves *low* in the clump. They are formed with two lazy daisy stitches pointing down from a central point and three lazy daisy stitches pointing upwards from the same point.

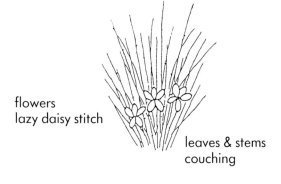

flowers
lazy daisy stitch

leaves & stems
couching

WINTER ROSE (PINK HELLEBORUS) *Helleborus orientalis*

THREADS
316   antique mauve — medium
3052   green grey — medium
3346   hunter green

STRANDS, STITCHES AND NEEDLES
flowers   2 strands 316, lazy daisy stitch, crewel 8
                       1 strand each 316 and 3052 blended, lazy daisy
                       stitch, crewel 8
leaves   1 strand each 3052 and 3346 blended, lazy daisy
                       stitch, crewel 8

Lightly mark a dome-shaped area. The pink and pink-green flowers are
worked first over the marked area, leaving space for the small leaves
above each flower. Work flowers with three lazy daisy stitches from
the same point, fanning downwards. Work leaves in the blended greens
with two small lazy daisy stitches pointing upward from the centre top
of the flowers. Cluster larger lazy daisy leaves densely around the base
and scatter a few leaves through the flowers, if appropriate.

flowers
lazy daisy stitch

leaves
lazy daisy stitch

WINTER ROSE (WHITE HELLEBORUS) *Helleborus niger*

THREADS
blanc neige
472   avocado green — ultra light
469   avocado green

STRANDS, STITCHES AND NEEDLES

flowers	2 strands blanc neige, lazy daisy stitch, crewel 8
	2 strands 472, lazy daisy stitch, crewel 8
	1 strand each blanc neige and 472 blended, lazy daisy stitch, crewel 8
leaves	2 strands 469, lazy daisy stitch, crewel 8

Lightly mark a dome-shaped area. The flowers in the three different combinations listed above (white, white-pale green and pale green) are worked first over the marked area, leaving space for the small leaves above each flower. Work the flowers with three lazy daisy stitches from the same point, fanning downwards. Work small leaves in the darker green with two lazy daisy stitches pointing upwards from the centre top of each flower. Cluster larger, lazy daisy leaves densely around the base and scatter a few leaves through the flowers, if appropriate.

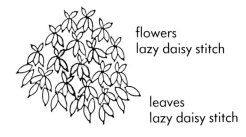

flowers
lazy daisy stitch

leaves
lazy daisy stitch

WISTERIA *Wisteria sinensis*

THREADS

208	lavender – very dark
210	lavender – medium
640	beige grey – very dark
3013	khaki green – light
3348	yellow green – medium

STRANDS, STITCHES AND NEEDLES

vine	2 strands 640, stem stitch, crewel 8
flower stalks	2 strands 3348, coral stitch, crewel 8
	2 strands 208, French knots, crewel 8
	1 strand each 208 and 210 blended, French knots, crewel 8
	3 strands 210, French knots, crewel 7
leaf stalks	2 strands 3348, coral stitch, crewel 8
leaves	1 strand each 3013 and 3348 blended, lazy daisy stitch crewel 8

Mark vine on pergola and work in coral stitch. Some of the coral stitch will be covered by flowers but the top 5mm (⅛") will form the stalk. The coral stitch knots will peep through the flowers.

Commence working the flowers at the tip and work upwards in French knots using the different thread combination as listed above, starting with 208. The bulk of the flowers will be worked in the three strands of 210. Make sure the flowers do not become too wide; they should be long and pendulous; they should not resemble bunches of grapes. Some people prefer to work these flowers form the top down to the tip.
The leaf stalks curve from the vine and are worked in coral stitch. The leaves are worked in pairs of lazy daisy stitches (nine to 11 leaves).

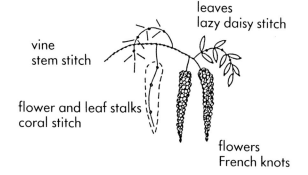

leaves
lazy daisy stitch

vine
stem stitch

flower and leaf stalks
coral stitch

flowers
French knots

ARCH

THREADS
319   pistachio green — very dark

STRANDS, STITCHES AND NEEDLES
arch   3 strands 319, whipped stem stitch, crewel 7
ornamentation   1 strand 319, stem stitch and straight stitch, crewel 9

Pencil in the arch and work the two rows of whipped stem stitch; take care not to stitch this too tightly. Work the decorative scroll on the top of the arch with stem stitch and the crossed bars with straight stitch; the bars can be couched where they cross.

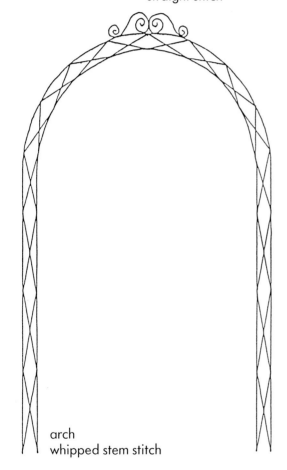

ornamentation
stem stitch
straight stitch

arch
whipped stem stitch

FLAGSTONES

THREADS
612   drab brown – medium

STRANDS, STITCHES AND NEEDLES
1 strand, stem stitch, crewel 9

Mark flagstones and work in 1 strand stem stitch

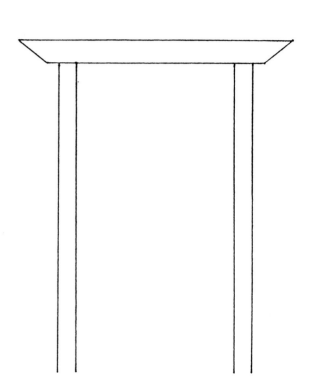

PERGOLA

THREADS
611   drab brown – dark

STRANDS, STITCHES AND NEEDLES
2 strands, stem stitch, crewel 8

Draw in outline of pergola and work in stem stitch. Flowers and leaves will cover come parts of the pergola.

Reference – Macoboy, S. Stirling Macoboy's *What Flower is That?* Weldon Publishing, 1989.

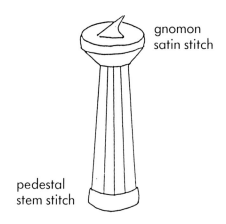

gnomon
satin stitch

pedestal
stem stitch

SUNDIAL

THREADS
842   beige brown — very light
415   pearl grey

STRANDS, STITCHES AND NEEDLES
pedestal   2 strands 842, stem stitch, crewel 8
gnomon*   2 strands 415, satin stitch, crewel 8

Draw the sundial and work the pedestal with stem stitch. Work the gnomon with satin stitch.

*the vertical, triangular plate of a sundial.

rim
satin stitch

outline
stem stitch

pot
long & short stitch

TERRACOTTA POT

THREADS
356   terracotta — medium

STRANDS, STITCHES AND NEEDLES
pot   2 strands 356, long and short stitch, crewel 8
rim   2 strands 356, satin stitch, crewel 8
outline   1 strand 356, stem stitch, crewel 9

Note: Use a small hoop for good tension when working long and short stitch.

Pencil in your terracotta pot and work in long and short stitch; start just below the rim and work downwards. Work the rim of the pot with a vertical satin stitch. To complete, outline the pot with stem stitch.

TUB

THREADS
840   beige brown — medium
839   beige brown — dark

STRANDS, STITCHES AND NEEDLES
timber slats   2 strands 840, satin stitch, crewel 8
hoops   2 strands 839, stem stitch, crewel 8
outline   2 strands 840, stem stitch, crewel 8

Lightly mark the tub. Work the three rows of timber slats with a vertical satin stitch. Work each of the three metal hoops with four rows of stem stitch. Outline the top and sides of the tub with one row of stem stitch.

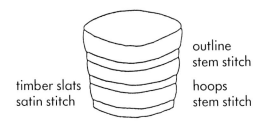

outline
stem stitch

timber slats
satin stitch

hoops
stem stitch

VERSAILLES PLANTER

THREADS
319   pistachio green — very dark

STRANDS, STITCHES AND NEEDLES
outline   2 strands 319, stem stitch, crewel 8
inside lines   2 strands 319, couching, crewel 8
knobs   2 strands 319, satin stitch, crewel 8

Lightly mark the planter and work the outline in stem stitch. Add the inside lines with couching and the knobs in satin stitch.

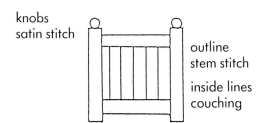

knobs
satin stitch

outline
stem stitch

inside lines
couching

BEE

THREADS
3371   black brown
972   canary — deep
762   pearl grey — very light

STRANDS, STITCHES AND NEEDLES

body	1 strand 972, satin stitch, crewel 9
	1 strand 3371, satin stitch and stem stitch, crewel 9
head	1 strand 3371, French knot (2 twists), crewel 9
wings	1 strand 762, buttonhole stitch, crewel 9

Draw the body of the bee. Work the five stripes each with three or four satin stitches. Start with the gold and alternate with the black brown. Outline the body with stem stitch and work the head with a French knot. Add a small tail with a straight stitch. Finally, embroider the wings, each with a half-circle of buttonhole stitch.

body
satin stitch
outline — stem stitch

wings
buttonhole stitch

head — French knot
tail — straight stitch

BUTTERFLY

THREADS

612	drab brown — medium	
727	topaz — very light	
840	beige brown — medium	

STRANDS, STITCHES AND NEEDLES

wings	outer	1 strand 612, buttonhole stitch, crewel 9
	inner	1 strand 727, buttonhole stitch, crewel 9
	sides	1 strand 840, straight stitch, crewel 9
spots		1 strand 840 French knot (2 twists), crewel 9
feelers		1 strand 840, French knot stalks, crewel 9
body		2 strands 840, bullion (13 wraps), straw 8

Carefully study the illustration and draw the butterfly with larger front wings and smaller back wings, each with an inner and outer part. Work the outer wings and then the inner wings with buttonhole stitch. Highlight the edges of the wings with a straight stitch and work a spot on each wing with a French knot. Add the feelers with French knot stalks. Starting at the head of the butterfly, embroider the body with a bullion stitch (13 wraps), couching in the centre.

Reference — Macoboy, S. *Stirling Macoboy's What Flower is That?* Weldon Publishing, 1989.

feelers
French knot stalks

spot
French knot

body
bullion stitch

wings
buttonhole stitch
sides — straight stitch

BUTTERFLY 2

THREADS

341   blue violet – light
452   shell grey – medium

STRANDS, STITCHES AND NEEDLES

wings   2 strands 341, long and short stitch, crewel 8
body   2 strands 452, bullion stitch, straw 8
feelers   1 strand 452, stem stitch, crewel 9
outline   1 strand 452, stem stitch, crewel 9

Draw outline of butterfly and work wings in long and short stitch. Work body between the wings in bullion stitch (13 wraps). Couch in position to form head and body. Outline wings in one strand 452 stem stitch and place feelers at top of head arching outwards.

feelers and outline
stem stitch

wings
long and short stitch

body
bullion stitch

PUSSY CAT

THREADS

452   shell grey – medium

STRANDS, STITCHES AND NEEDLES

Body   2 strands, long and short stitch. crewel 8
Head   2 strands, satin stitch, crewel 8
Tail   2 strands, stem stitch, crewel 8
Ears   2 strands, satin stitch, crewel 8
Outline   1 strand, stem stitch, crewel 9

Draw a simple outline of a cat. Work body in long and short stitch, head and ears in satin stitch and long tail tapering to a point in two rows stem stitch. Outline body and head in 1 strand stem stitch.

head
satin stitch

body
long and short stitch

outline
stem stitch

tail
stem stitch

SNAIL

THREADS

612   drab brown – medium
420   hazelnut brown – dark
762   pearl grey – very light

STRANDS, STITCHES AND NEEDLES

shell   1 strand each 612 and 420 blended, stem stitch,
                    crewel 8
head and tail   1 strand 420, straight stitch, crewel 9
feelers   1 strand 420, French knot stalk, crewel 9
trail   1 strand 762, stem and running stitch, crewel 9

Work shell in stem stitch starting in the centre and work around in an anti-clockwise direction until a small spiral of desired size is achieved. Work head and tail in straight stitch and feelers on top of head in French knot stalk. Work trail leading away from snail in stem stitch with a few running stitches tapering off into the foliage. Remember that the snail is very small.

shell
stem stitch

feelers
French knot stalks

trail
stem and running stitches

body
straight stitch

SPIDER AND WEB

THREADS

762   pearl grey – light
611   drab brown – dark

STRANDS, STITCHES AND NEEDLES

web   1 strand 762, straight and stem stitch, crewel 9 spider   head   1 strand 611, French knots, 2 twists, crewel 9

body   1 strand 611, lazy daisy stitch, crewel 9

legs   1 strand 611, straight stitch

Find a suitable position for the web where the spokes can attach to the foliage or flowers. Work eight spokes in long straight stitches crossing over in the centre; couch at this point. Work a long stem stitch over each of the spokes in a circular manner. The number of times this is done depends on the size of the web – do at least three.

The spider is very tiny. Work the head first in one French knot (two twists) and the body in a lazy daisy stitch. Place eight legs in straight stitch, four on either side of the head.

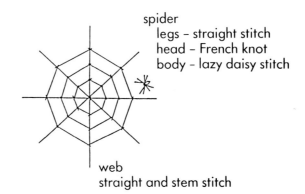

spider
  legs – straight stitch
  head – French knot
  body – lazy daisy stitch

web
straight and stem stitch

Embroidery stitches have many different names and feature variations in structure and technique of working. This glossary describes how the stitches have been worked for the designs in this book.

For left-handed embroiderers, instructions follow the right-handed embroiderers section.

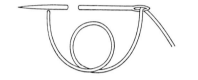

Stem or outline stitch

STEM OR OUTLINE STITCH

A simple stitch for stems, outlines and filling.

Working from left to right, take small, even straight or slightly slanting stitches along the design line. Leave a space between the point where the needle emerges and the previous stitch. Keep the thread below or on the same side of your work. for wide stem stitch, make the stitches on a greater angle.

WHIPPED STEM STITCH

Whipped stem stitch gives a corded effect.

Work a row of stem stitch along the design line and bring the needle to the top of your work. Work in the opposite direction to that of the stem stitch. With the blunt end of the needle whip back through each stem stitch, but not into the fabric.

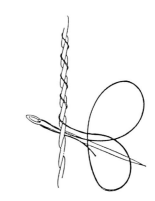

Whipped stem stitch

COUCHING

The branches and flower stems in this book worked in couching have one or two strands of thread laid down and one strand for the tying stitch of matching thread. The use of a small hoop will help with tension. Use two needles and keep them on top of your work to prevent tangling. Anchor the thread not in use and keep it out of the way. Short stems in couching can be worked with one needle and thread.

Lay the thread along the design line, holding and guiding its direction with your thumb. Tie it down with small straight stitches made at regular intervals.

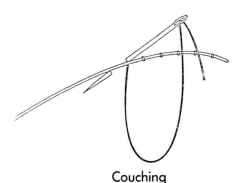

Couching

CORAL STITCH

Coral stitch is a simple knotted line stitch useful for flower stems.

Hold the thread to the left along the design line. Take a small stitch towards you with the thread over and around the needle; pull through forming a knot. Continue at regular intervals.

Coral stitch

FRENCH KNOTS

When working French knots you will have more control and be able to develop a rhythm if a small (10 cm/4″) hoop is used. To increase the size of knots, use more strands of thread.

Bring the thread up at the desired spot. Hold the thread firmly with your left hand. With the needle pointing toward you, place it under the thread from the left-hand side and twist it around once. Insert the needle close to where the thread first emerged, but not in the same hole. Draw the thread around the needle to firm the knot and pull through to the back. Pass on to the position for the next knot.

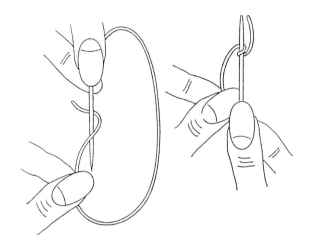

French knots

FRENCH KNOT STALKS

French knot stalks are worked in the same manner as French knots. The use of a small embroidery hoop will help you achieve good tension.

To form the stalk, after encircling the needle with the thread, insert the needle the desired distance away from where it first emerged. Pull through to the back and pass on to the position for the next stitch.

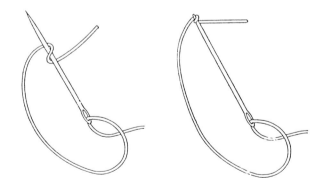

French knot stalks

COLONIAL KNOTS OR CANDLEWICKING KNOTS

This stitch differs from a French knot in that the twists are worked in a figure of eight. It stands up high on the fabric and needs to be worked very firmly. You will have more control and be able to develop a rhythm if a small (10 cm/4″) hoop is used.

Bring the thread up at the desired spot. Hold the thread firmly with your left hand. With the needle pointing away from you, place it under the thread from the left-hand side and twist it in an anti-clockwise direction away from you. The needle will now be facing you. The second part of the stitch is the same as a French knot. Now place the needle under the thread from the left-hand side and twist it around once back to the original position.

Insert the needle close to where the thread first emerged, but not in the same hole. Draw the thread around the shaft of the needle to firm the knot and pull through to the back. Pass on to the position for the next knot.

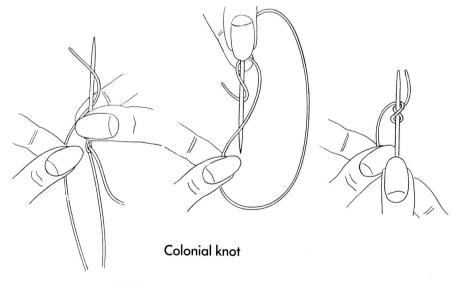

Colonial knot

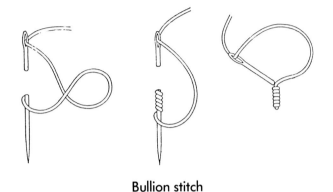

Bullion stitch

BULLION STITCH

This stitch should be worked with a straw or millinery needle. The small eye will allow the needle to pass easily through the wraps. The number of wraps should equal the length of the back stitch.

Commence as though to make a back stitch the required length for the bullion stitch. Bring the needle up at the starting point but do not pull through. Wrap the thread around the needle, in a clockwise direction, the required number of times. Do not wrap too tightly. Place your left thumb over the wraps, then pull the needle through the wraps. As you pull the thread up firmly, the bullion will turn back. Adjust the wraps if necessary. Insert the needle at the starting point and pull through to complete the bullion stitch.

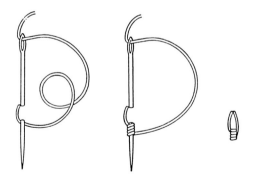

Lazy daisy bullion stitch

LAZY DAISY BULLION STITCH

This stitch is a combination of lazy daisy and bullion stitches. It is useful for leaves and flower petals and gives an interesting texture. It should be worked with a straw needle.

Bring the needle through at the point where you wish to begin your stitch. Hold the thread below your work and insert the needle close to where the thread first emerged. Bring the needle out at the desired distance, as though you are making a small lazy daisy stitch, keeping the thread underneath. Do not pull the needle through at this stage. Wrap the thread around the needle three to five times (or desired number) in an anti-clockwise direction. Place your left thumb over the wraps, then pull the needle and the thread firmly through the wraps. To anchor the stitch insert the needle at the tip of the bullion and pull through to the back of the fabric. Pass on to the beginning of the next stitch. Be sure to work each stitch the same to ensure that the long stitch down the side lies on the same side.

LAZY DAISY OR DETACHED CHAIN

This is a very useful stitch for leaves and flower petals.

Bring the needle through at the point where you wish to begin your stitch. Hold the thread below your work and insert the needle to the right, close to where the thread first emerged. Bring the needle out at the desired distance, keeping the thread underneath. Fasten the loop at the end with a small straight stitch. Pass on to the beginning of the next stitch.

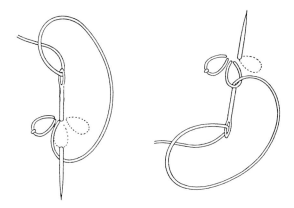

Lazy daisy or detached chain

DOUBLE LAZY DAISY STITCH

This stitch is useful for leaves and large flower petals. It can be worked in two colours.

The inside stitch is worked first as an ordinary lazy daisy stitch. The larger second stitch is worked outside and around the first stitch.

Double lazy daisy stitch

FLY STITCH

Fly stitch is an open lazy daisy stitch. The tying stitch can vary in length as required. It can be worked singly, vertically, horizontally or radiating into a circle.

Bring the thread through at the top left of your design line. Insert the needle a little distance away to the right and take a small diagonal stitch to the centre with the thread below the needle. Pull through and fasten with a straight downward stitch.

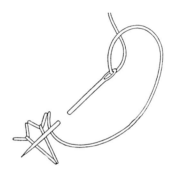

Fly stitch

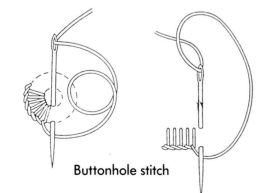

Buttonhole stitch

BUTTONHOLE STITCH

This stitch is the same as blanket stitch but the stitches are worked closer together. It can be worked in a row or a circle.

Start on the outside edge and work from left to right. Hold the thread below and take a downward straight stitch and draw up with the thread underneath the needle. Continue in this way, spacing stitches as required.

SATIN STITCH-SLANTED

This stitch should be worked with even stitches to cover the fabric completely, resulting in a smooth finish. Work with a stabbing motion for better tension. The use of a hoop will help.

A running stitch may be worked first to outline the design. This will help to form a good edge. Work slanting stitches closely together across the area outlined.

STRAIGHT STITCH

Straight stitch is a single satin stitch and can be worked in any direction and to any length. The use of a small embroidery hoop will help you achieve good tension. Do not make the stitches too long, as snagging may occur.

LONG AND SHORT SATIN STITCH

This stitch can be used to fill areas too large to be covered by satin stitch. It can also be used to achieve subtle shading. The use of a small embroidery hoop will help you achieve good tension.

Work the first row in alternate long and short satin stitches. Closely follow the outline of the design shape. The following rows are then worked in long stitches in a 'brick' fashion until the area is filled. The gaps in the final row will be filled with short stitches.

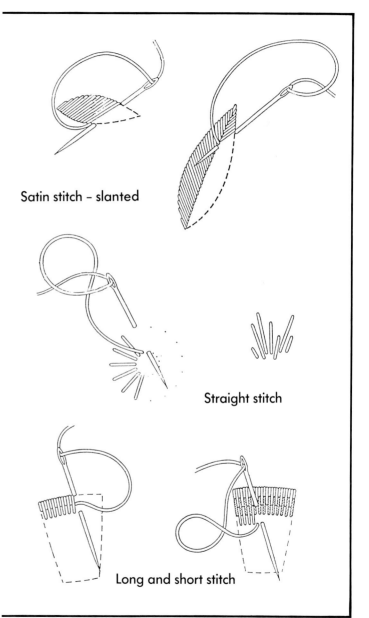

Satin stitch - slanted

Straight stitch

Long and short stitch

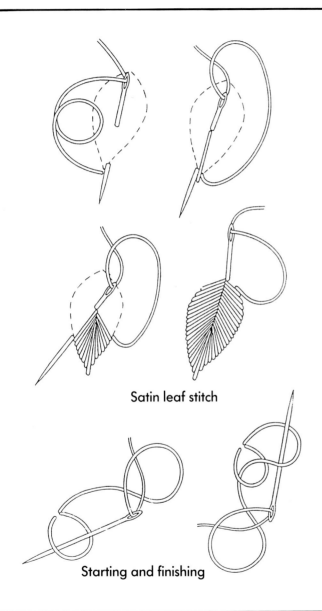

Satin leaf stitch

Starting and finishing

SATIN LEAF STITCH

This variation of satin stitch is easy to work and forms a very realistic leaf. It is taken from Brazilian embroidery.

The first stitch should be a little longer than you might expect, in order to form a good point on the leaf. Work the first satin stitch from the point of the leaf back into the centre of the leaf. Bring the needle back up on the right of the first stitch at the leaf tip. Take this second stitch back to the central leaf vein and insert the needle just below, but very close to the first stitch. Work the satin stitches alternately from each side, fanning them as the leaf forms. At the same time, continue to work closely down the central vein. You may need to add one or two extra stitches on one side of your leaf if it is not symmetrical.

STARTING AND FINISHING

The use of a small knot is quite an acceptable and secure way to begin your work.

There are many satisfactory ways to finish off your thread. The following method is used for smocking and is neat and secure.

Take a small stitch to form a loop. Pass the needle through the loop to form a second loop. Pass the needle through the second loop and pull up tightly to form a secure knot.

STITCH GLOSSARY (left-handed)

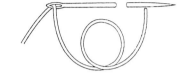

STEM OR OUTLINE STITCH

A simple stitch for stems, outlines and filling.

Working from right to left, take small, even straight or slightly slanting stitches along the design line. Leave a space between the point where the needle emerges and the previous stitch. Keep the thread below or on the same side of your work. For wide stem stitch, make the stitches on a greater angle.

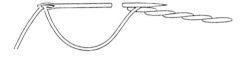

Stem or outline stitch

WHIPPED STEM STITCH

Whipped stem stitch gives a corded effect.

Work a row of stem stitch along the design line and bring the needle to the top of your work. Work in the opposite direction to that of the stem stitch. With the blunt end of the needle whip back through each stem stitch, but not into the fabric.

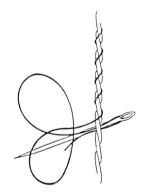

Whipped stem stitch

COUCHING

The branches and flower stems in this book worked in couching have one or two strands of thread laid down and one strand for the tying stitch of matching thread. The use of a small hoop will help with tension. Use two needles and keep them on top of your work to prevent tangling. Anchor the thread not in use and keep it out of the way. Short stems in couching can be worked with one needle and thread.

Lay the thread along the design line, holding and guiding its direction with your thumb. Tie it down with small straight stitches made at regular intervals.

CORAL STITCH

Coral stitch is a simple knotted line stitch useful for flower stems.

Hold the thread to the right along the design line. Take a small stitch towards you with the thread over and around the needle; pull through forming a knot. Continue at regular intervals.

FRENCH KNOTS

When working French knots you will have more control and be able to develop a rhythm if a small (10 cm/4″) hoop is used. To increase the size of knots, use more strands of thread.

Bring the thread up at the desired spot. Hold the thread firmly with your right hand. With the needle pointing toward you, place it under the thread from the right-hand side and twist it around once. Insert the needle close to where the thread first emerged, but not in the same hole. Draw the thread around the needle to firm the knot and pull through to the back. Pass on to the position for the next knot.

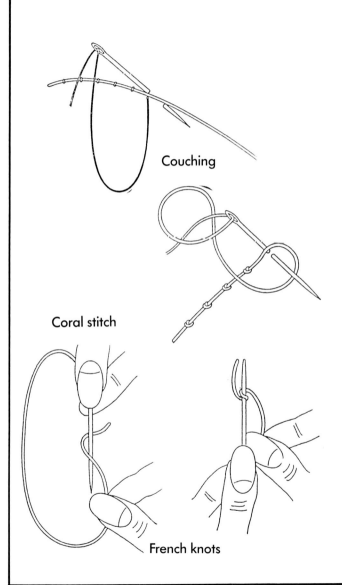

Couching

Coral stitch

French knots

FRENCH KNOT STALKS

French knot stalks are worked in the same manner as French knots. The use of a small embroidery hoop will help you achieve good tension.

To form the stalk, after encircling the needle with the thread, insert the needle the desired distance away from where it first emerged. Pull through to the back and pass on to the position for the next stitch.

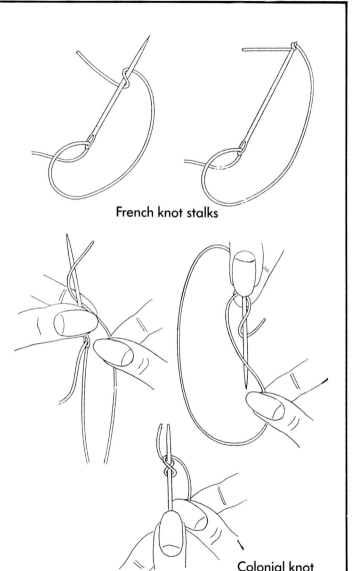

French knot stalks

COLONIAL KNOTS OR CANDLEWICKING KNOTS

This stitch differs from a French knot in that the twists are worked in a figure of eight. It stands up high on the fabric and needs to be worked very firmly. You will have more control and be able to develop a rhythm if a small (10 cm/4") hoop is used.

Bring the thread up at the desired spot. Hold the thread firmly with your right hand. With the needle pointing away from you, place it under the thread from the right-hand side and twist it in a clockwise direction away from you. The needle will now be facing you. The second part of the stitch is the same as a French knot. Now place the needle under the thread from the right-hand side and twist it around once back to the original position.

Insert the needle close to where the thread first emerged, but not in the same hole. Draw the thread around the shaft of the needle to firm the knot and pull through to the back. Pass on to the position for the next knot.

Colonial knot

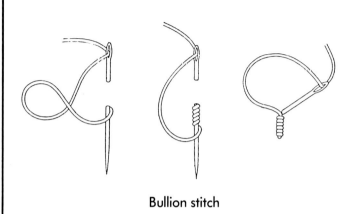

Bullion stitch

BULLION STITCH

This stitch should be worked with a straw or millinery needle. The small eye will allow the needle to pass easily through the wraps. The number of wraps should equal the length of the back stitch.

Commence as though to make a back stitch the required length for the bullion stitch. Bring the needle up at the starting point but do not pull through. Wrap the thread around the needle, in an anti-clockwise direction, the required number of times. Do not wrap too tightly. Place your right thumb over the wraps, then pull the needle through the wraps. As you pull the thread up firmly, the bullon will turn back. Adjust the wraps if necessary. Insert the needle at the starting point and pull through to complete the bullion stitch.

LAZY DAISY BULLION STITCH

This stitch is a combination of lazy daisy and bullion stitches. It is useful for leaves and flower petals and gives an interesting texture. It should be worked with a straw needle.

Bring the needle through at the point where you wish to begin your stitch. Hold the thread below your work and insert the needle close to where the thread first emerged. Bring the needle out at the desired distance, as though you are making a small lazy daisy stitch, keeping the thread underneath. Do not pull the needle through at this stage. Wrap the thread around the needle three to five times (or desired number) in a clockwise direction. Place your right thumb over the wraps, then pull the needle and the thread firmly through the wraps. To anchor the stitch insert the needle at the tip of the bullion and pull through to the back of the fabric. Pass on to the beginning of the next stitch. Be sure to work each stitch the same to ensure that the long stitch down the side lies on the same side.

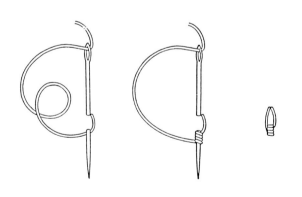

Lazy daisy bullion stitch

LAZY DAISY OR DETACHED CHAIN

This is a very useful stitch for leaves and flower petals.

Bring the needle through at the point where you wish to begin your stitch. Hold the thread below your work and insert the needle to the left, close to where the thread first emerged. Bring the needle out at the desired distance, keeping the thread underneath. Fasten the loop at the end with a small straight stitch. Pass on to the beginning of the next stitch.

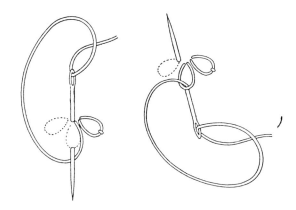

Lazy daisy or detached chain

DOUBLE LAZY DAISY STITCH

This stitch is useful for leaves and large flower petals. It can be worked in two colours.

The inside stitch is worked first as an ordinary lazy daisy stitch. The larger second stitch is worked outside and around the first stitch.

Double lazy daisy stitch

FLY STITCH

Fly stitch is an open lazy daisy stitch. The tying stitch can vary in length as required. It can be worked singly, vertically, horizontally or radiating into a circle.

Bring the thread through at the top right of your design line. Insert the needle a little distance away to the left and take a small diagonal stitch to the centre with the thread below the needle. Pull through and fasten with a straight downward stitch.

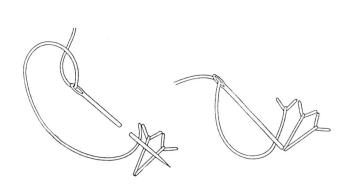

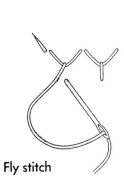

Fly stitch

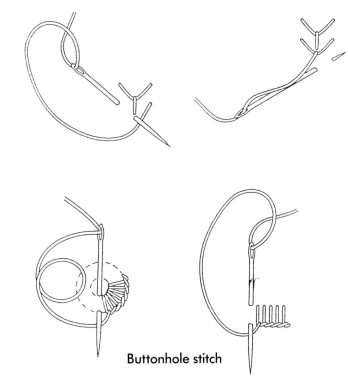

Buttonhole stitch

BUTTONHOLE STITCH

This stitch is the same as blanket stitch but the stitches are worked closer together. It can be worked in a row or a circle.

Start on the outside edge and work from right to left. Hold the thread below and take a downward straight stitch and draw up with the thread underneath the needle. Continue in this way, spacing stitches as required.

SATIN STITCH-SLANTED

This stitch should be worked with even stitches to cover the fabric completely, resulting in a smooth finish. Work with a stabbing motion for better tension. The use of a hoop will help.

A running stitch may be worked first to outline the design. This will help to form a good edge. Work slanting stitches closely together across the area outlined.

STRAIGHT STITCH

Straight stitch is a single satin stitch and can be worked in any direction and to any length. The use of a small embroidery hoop will help you achieve good tension. Do not make the stitches too long, as snagging may occur.

LONG AND SHORT SATIN STITCH

This stitch can be used to fill areas too large to be covered by satin stitch. It can also be used to achieve subtle shading. The use of a small embroidery hoop will help you achieve good tension.

Work the first row in alternate long and short satin stitches. Closely follow the outline of the design shape. The following rows are then worked in long stitches in a 'brick' fashion until the area is filled. The gaps in the final row will be filled with short stitches.

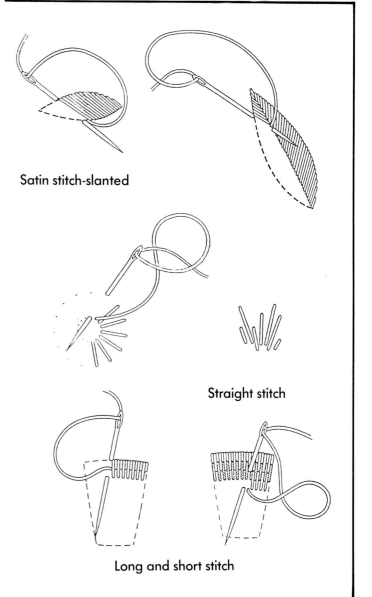

Satin stitch-slanted

Straight stitch

Long and short stitch

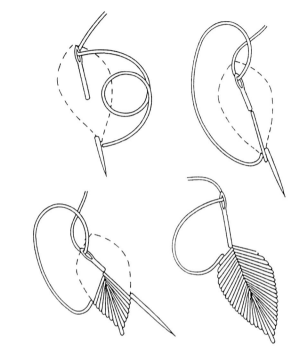

Satin leaf stitch

SATIN LEAF STITCH

This variation of satin stitch is easy to work and forms a very realistic leaf. It is taken from Brazilian embroidery.

The first stitch should be a little longer than you might expect, in order to form a good point on the leaf. Work the first satin stitch from the point of the leaf back into the centre of the leaf. Bring the needle back up on the left of the first stitch at the leaf tip. Take this second stitch back to the central leaf vein and insert the needle just below, but very close to the first stitch. Work the satin stitches alternately from each side, fanning them as the leaf forms. At the same time, continue to work closely down the central vein. You may need to add one or two extra stitches on one side of your leaf if it is not symmetrical.

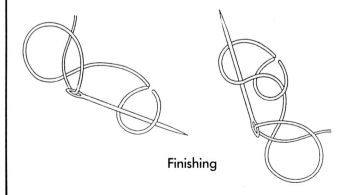

Finishing

STARTING AND FINISHING

The use of a small knot is quite an acceptable and secure way to begin your work.

There are many satisfactory ways to finish off your thread. The following method is used for smocking and is neat and secure.

Take a small stitch to form a loop. Pass the needle through the loop to form a second loop. Pass the needle through the second loop and pull up tightly to form a secure knot.

DMC STRANDED COTTON AND
COLOUR NAMES IN NUMERICAL ORDER

white	blanc neige	316	antique mauve — medium
ecru		317	pewter grey
208	lavender — very dark	318	steel grey — light
209	lavender — dark	319	pistachio green — very dark
210	lavender — medium	320	pistachio green — medium
211	lavender — light	321	Christmas red
221	shell pink — very dark	322	navy blue — very light
223	shell pink — light	326	rose — very deep
224	shell pink — very light	327	violet — very dark
225	shell pink — ultra very light	333	blue violet — very dark
300	mahogany — very dark	334	baby blue — medium
301	mahogany — medium	335	rose
304	Christmas red — medium	336	navy blue
307	lemon	340	blue violet — medium
309	rose — deep	341	blue violet — light
310	black	347	salmon — very dark
311	navy blue — medium	349	coral — dark
312	navy blue — light	350	coral — medium
315	antique mauve — very dark	351	coral

352	coral — light	498	Christmas red — dark	605	cranberry — very light
353	peach flesh	500	blue green — very dark	606	bright orange-red
355	terracotta — dark	501	blue green — dark	608	bright orange
356	terracotta — medium	502	blue green	610	drab brown — very dark
367	pistachio green — dark	503	blue green — medium	611	drab brown — dark
368	pistachio green — light	504	blue green — light	612	drab brown — medium
369	pistachio green — very light	517	wedgwood — medium	613	drab brown — light
370	mustard — medium	518	wedgwood — light	632	desert sand — ultra very dark
371	mustard	519	sky blue	640	beige grey — very dark
372	mustard — light	520	fern green — dark	642	beige grey — dark
400	mahogany — dark	522	fern green	644	beige grey — medium
402	mahogany — very light	523	fern green — light	645	beaver grey — very dark
407	sportsman flesh — dark	524	fern green — very light	646	beaver grey — dark
413	pewter grey — dark	535	ash grey — very light	647	beaver grey — medium
414	steel grey — dark	543	beige brown — ultra very light	648	beaver grey — light
415	pearl grey	550	violet — very dark	666	Christmas red — bright
420	hazelnut brown — dark	552	violet — medium	676	old gold — light
422	hazelnut brown — light	553	violet	677	old gold — very light
433	brown — medium	554	violet — light	680	old gold — dark
434	brown — light	561	jade — very dark	699	Christmas green
435	brown — very light	562	jade — medium	700	Christmas green — bright
436	tan	563	jade — light	701	Christmas green — light
437	tan — light	564	jade — very light	702	kelly green
444	lemon — dark	580	moss green — dark	703	chartreuse
445	lemon — light	581	moss green	704	chartreuse — bright
451	shell grey — dark	597	turquoise	712	cream
452	shell grey — medium	598	turquoise — light	718	plum
453	shell grey — light	600	cranberrry — very dark	720	orange spice — dark
469	avocado green	601	cranberry — dark	721	orange spice — medium
470	avocado green — light	602	cranberry — medium	722	orange spice — light
471	avocado green — very light	603	cranberry	725	topaz
472	avocado green — ultra light	604	cranberry — light	726	topaz — light

727	topaz — very light	793	cornflower blue — medium	838	beige brown — very dark
729	old gold — medium	794	cornflower blue — light	839	beige brown — dark
730	olive green — very dark	796	royal blue — dark	840	beige brown — medium
731	olive green — dark	797	royal blue	841	beige brown — light
732	olive green	798	delft — dark	842	beige brown — very light
733	olive green — medium	799	delft — medium	844	beaver grey — ultra dark
734	olive green — light	800	delft — pale	869	hazelnut brown — very dark
738	tan — very light	801	coffee brown — dark	890	pistachio green — ultra dark
739	tan — ultra very light	806	peacock blue — dark	891	carnation — dark
740	tangerine	807	peacock blue	892	carnation — medium
741	tangerine — medium	809	delft	893	carnation — light
742	tangerine — light	813	blue — light	894	carnation — very light
743	yellow — medium	814	garnet — dark	895	hunter green — very dark
744	yellow — pale	815	garnet — medium	898	coffee brown — very dark
745	yellow — light pale	816	garnet	899	rose — medium
746	off white	817	coral red — very dark	900	burnt orange — dark
747	sky blue — very light	818	baby pink	902	garnet — very dark
754	peach flesh — light	819	baby pink — light	904	parrot green — very dark
758	terracotta — very light	820	royal blue — very dark	905	parrot green — dark
760	salmon	822	beige grey — light	906	parrot green — medium
761	salmon — light	823	navy blue — dark	907	parrot green — light
762	pearl grey — very light	824	blue — very dark	909	emerald green — very dark
772	yellow green — very light	825	blue — dark	910	emerald green — dark
775	baby blue — very light	826	blue — medium	911	emerald green — medium
776	pink — medium	827	blue — very light	912	emerald green — light
778	antique mauve — very light	828	blue — ultra very light	913	Nile green — medium
780	topaz — ultra very dark	829	golden olive — very dark	915	plum — dark
781	topaz — very dark	830	golden olive — dark	917	plum — medium
782	topaz — dark	831	golden olive — medium	918	red copper — dark
783	topaz — medium	832	golden olive	919	red copper
791	cornflower blue — very dark	833	golden olive — light	920	copper — medium
792	cornflower blue — dark	834	golden olive — very light	921	copper

922	copper — light	970	pumpkin — light	3052	green grey — medium
924	grey green — very dark	971	pumpkin	3053	green grey
926	grey green — medium	972	canary — deep	3064	sportsman flesh — very dark
927	grey green — light	973	canary — bright	3072	beaver grey — very light
928	grey green — very light	975	golden brown — dark	3078	golden yellow — very light
930	antique blue — dark	976	golden brown — medium	3325	baby blue — light
931	antique blue — medium	977	golden brown — light	3326	rose — light
932	antique blue — light	986	forest green — very dark	3328	salmon — dark
934	black avocado green	987	forest green — dark	3340	apricot — medium
935	avocado green — dark	988	forest green — medium	3341	apricot
936	avocado green — very dark	989	forest green	3345	hunter green — dark
937	avocado green — medium	991	aquamarine — dark	3346	hunter green
938	coffee brown — ultra dark	992	aquamarine	3347	yellow green — medium
939	navy blue — very dark	993	aquamarine — light	3348	yellow green — light
943	aquamarine — medium	995	electric blue — dark	3350	dusty rose — ultra dark
945	sportsman flesh — medium	996	electric blue — medium	3354	dusty rose — light
946	burnt orange — medium	3011	khaki green — dark	3362	pine green — dark
947	burnt orange	3012	khaki green — medium	3363	pine green — medium
948	peach flesh — very light	3013	khaki green — light	3364	pine green
950	sportsman flesh	3021	brown grey — very dark	3371	black brown
951	sportsman flesh — very light	3022	brown grey — medium	3607	plum — light
954	Nile green	3023	brown grey — light	3608	plum — very light
955	Nile green — light	3024	brown grey — very light	3609	plum — ultra light
956	geranium	3031	mocha brown — very dark	3685	mauve — dark
957	geranium — pale	3032	mocha brown — medium	3687	mauve
958	seagreen — dark	3033	mocha brown — very light	3688	mauve — medium
959	seagreen — medium	3041	antique violet — medium	3689	mauve — light
961	dusty rose — dark	3042	antique violet — light	3705	melon — dark
962	dusty rose — medium	3045	yellow beige — dark	3706	melon — medium
963	dusty rose — ultra very light	3046	yellow beige — medium	3708	melon — light
964	seagreen — light	3047	yellow beige — light	3712	salmon — medium
966	baby green — medium	3051	green grey — dark	3713	salmon — very light

3716	dusty rose — very light	3761	sky blue — very light
3721	shell pink — dark	3765	peacock blue — very dark
3722	shell pink — medium	3766	peacock blue — light
3726	antique mauve — dark	3768	grey green — dark
3727	antique mauve — light	3770	flesh — very light
3731	dusty rose — very dark	3772	negro flesh
3733	dusty rose	3773	sportsman flesh — medium
3740	antique violet — dark	3774	sportsman flesh — very light
3743	antique violet — very light	3776	mahogany — light
3746	blue violet — dark	3777	terracotta — very dark
3747	blue violet — very light	3778	terracotta — light
3750	antique blue — very dark	3779	terracotta — ultra very light
3752	antique blue — very light	3781	mocha brown — dark
3753	antique blue — ultra very light	3782	mocha brown — light
3755	baby blue	3787	brown grey — dark
3756	baby blue — ultra very light	3790	beige grey — ultra dark
3760	wedgwood — light	3799	pewter grey — very dark

FINISHING TOUCHES

Whaen you have finished placing all the plants and features, appraise your composition carefully for balance of colour, intensity and form. You will probably find you wish to add an extra flower or a few leaves here and there. Be sure at this stage to add your name or initials and the year. This is important because you have created a unique piece of fine art which will be valued by generations to come.

When you are completely happy with the balance of your work, it's time for the final touches!

- Tidy up the threads at the back, trimming back so there are no long tags.

- Carefully handwash your finished work in warm water with soft soap. (Do not soak as some threads may bleed.) Any stubborn pencil marks can be removed with a toothbrush.

- Rinse in distilled water. This will ensure that your heirloom embroidery will not discolour over the years. (Distilled water does not contain the acids and minerals found in tap water that cause brown stains in future years.) Do not wring out the embroidery because the creases can be very difficult to remove.

- It is best to iron your embroidery as soon as it is washed. Place a towel on the ironing board and overlay with a faded linen tea towel (so the dye will not run). Place the wet embroidery face down on the towels. You can either place another tea towel over the embroidery, or iron it direct, but *please* take care not to scorch it. While ironing, make sure you press any thread tags back over the embroidered part so that they don't show through the linen when the work is framed.

Now for the exciting bit! When you turn the embroidery over you will be thrilled to see your garden come to life. The pressure applied to the towels will have made the flowers stand out without showing indentations. Examine your work in daylight to ensure the finished piece is to your satisfaction in every detail.

After you have finished ironing your embroidery keep it flat in a folder until you take it to the framer. Arrange framing as soon as possible after washing and ironing.

The final decision you will need to make will concern the type and colour of the mount and frame. Choose a mount that complements your embroidered garden. In my season embroideries, I have chosen colours which reflect the feeling of the particular season: dull red for Winter, camel for Autumn and deep green for Summer. A good framer will help you make your choice.

If you are planning to do more than one season, make sure the frame you choose for the first garden will be available for the later ones.